A Student's Guide to

T. S. ELIOT

Naomi Pasachoff

Enslow Publishers, Inc.
40 Industrial Road
Box 398
Berkeley Heights, NJ 07922
USA
http://www.enslow.com

Library of Congress Cataloging-in-Publication Data

Pasachoff, Naomi E.
  A student's guide to T.S. Eliot / Naomi Pasachoff.
    p. cm.—(Understanding literature)
  Summary: "An introduction to the work of T.S. Eliot for high school students, which includes relevant biographical background on the author, explanations of various literary devices and techniques, and literary criticism for the novice reader"—Provided by publisher.
  Includes bibliographical references and index.
  ISBN-13: 978-0-7660-2881-4
  ISBN-10: 0-7660-2881-X
  1. Eliot, T. S. (Thomas Stearns), 1888-1965—Criticism and interpretation—Juvenile literature. I. Title.
  PS3509.L43Z8115 2008
  821'.912—dc22
                            2007024531

Printed in the United States of America

10 9 8 7 6 5 4 3 2 1

Dedication

In memory of Peter Lipton (1954–2007)
Like Eliot, an American philosopher
transplanted to England

CONTENTS

PREFACE

O ver the past dozen years or so, since I began writing short book-length biographies, I have had the pleasure of immersing myself in the lives of about a dozen fascinating individuals known for their contributions to science, politics, and/or literature. T. S. Eliot is the first of these subjects with whom I actually sat in the same room.

I was hardly the only person in the room, of course. My mother and I had gone, along with many others, to hear the great poet read from his own work. I do not remember the year of the event, but my high-school-girl excitement at catching a glimpse of Eliot and hearing his voice are quite vivid in my mind.

I remember, too, reading the news of Eliot's death in the obituary pages of *The New York Times* in January 1965. A freshman at Barnard College at the time, I wrote what I hoped was a witty letter to my older sister, a graduate student in English literature at Yale University, whom I greatly admired. Having recently seen the movie *It's a Hard Day's Night*, I recall that my lament on the occasion of the poet's death included the Beatles' memorable phrase, "He was a clean old gentleman." The following year at Barnard, I was privileged to study Eliot's "Prufrock" and *The Waste Land* with Professor Joann Ryan Morse (1930–2004), one of the greatest of many wonderful teachers with whom I would study literature over the next decade.

In 1966–67, as an English major at Radcliffe College (then the women's undergraduate institution whose students attended classes together with the men of Harvard College), I took a year-long tutorial devoted to the work of T. S. Eliot, taught by Edward Moore (now professor emeritus of English at Grinnell College). In preparing for the book now in your hands, I had the opportunity to reread the numerous annotations I made that year in the margins of the 1962 edition of Eliot's *Complete Poems and Plays*.

Also in 1966–67, as part of my extracurricular involvement with the Phillips Brooks House Association, the oldest and largest volunteer public service organization at Harvard, I made a weekly trip to a public school in Roxbury—center of the African-American community in Boston—along with other volunteers in the Roxbury Reading Program. I remember reading to the students from *Old Possum's Book of Practical Cats*. I thought of them when I first saw *Cats* with my husband and children in 1985. I wonder sometimes how many of those students also went to see the musical and whether any who did made the link to the poems they read with me in 1966.

When I was invited some forty years later to write *A Student's Guide to T. S. Eliot*, I jumped at the chance to read widely in the biographical and critical material that had proliferated since I first heard and read Eliot's work. I hope the students who read this book will enjoy their engagement with Eliot's poems, plays, and criticism as much as I have over the years, and will benefit from the opportunity to read that work in the context of his life as presented here.

POET OF HIS CENTURY?

An Introduction to the Life and Works of T. S. Eliot

On April 30, 1956, fourteen thousand people gathered in the basketball arena of the University of Minnesota in Minneapolis. They were there not to see athletes compete or to hear a concert. Were all those assembled in the sports arena really eager to hear a sixty-seven-year-old poet lecture on "The Frontiers of Criticism"? More likely, they flocked to the stadium merely to be in the presence of this larger-than-life man, T. S. Eliot.

Nor was the phenomenon limited to the English-speaking world. In Rome in 1958 to receive an honorary degree, Eliot found the city streets mobbed by so many young people shouting "Long live Eliot!" that the car in which he was driving had trouble reaching its destination.

THE POET AS ROCK STAR

In the 1950s Eliot's fame was greater than that of an ordinary poet or critic, greater even than that of other Nobel laureates in literature. His 1922 poem *The Waste*

Land had become a metaphor for the modern age. More than forty years following the publication of his 1915 poem "The Love Song of J. Alfred Prufrock," readers young and old still found it to be what one called "the authoritative statement about living in the modern world."[1] These poems changed the nature of British and American literature. They helped launch the modernist movement in literature. Modernist poetry like Eliot's "replaced the logical exposition of thoughts with collages of fragmentary images and complex allusions."[2] Eliot was also a successful playwright whose plays packed theatres in London and New York, a literary critic whose opinions affected the reputations of authors ancient and modern, and an influential editor who helped launch the careers of younger poets.

Eliot drew large audiences wherever he went. Among the many students who flocked to hear Eliot speak on "Poetry and Drama" at Harvard University on November 21, 1950, was seventeen-year-old Helen Hennessy, who grew up to be a noted critic. Despite the fact that she was ill with pneumonia, Hennessy considered herself lucky to be able to sit on the floor of the unheated Memorial Hall. Twenty-one years later she recalled being thrilled, along with others who had failed to find space in the university's Sanders Theatre, to hear Eliot's lecture "piped through" and "to catch a glimpse of the author of 'The Waste Land.'"[3]

11

RE-EVALUATING THE PUBLIC ICON

Eliot did not especially like being a public icon. More than once, he expressed his uneasiness about his hold on the popular imagination. He complained to one interviewer about having "become a myth, a fabulous creature that doesn't exist."[4] Days after his Harvard appearance in 1950, he expressed disappointment to a friend because "No one thinks of me as a poet any more, but as a celebrity."[5]

Despite his dissatisfaction with his cult status, how would Eliot have reacted if he knew how young Helen Hennessy's view of him would change? In 1971, only six years after Eliot's death at the age of seventy-six, Hennessy, now Helen Vendler, a leading American critic of poetry, harshly summed up Eliot's achievement in a front-page article in *The New York Times Book Review:* "The career tailed off more disastrously than any other in living memory, with only sporadic lines reminding a reader of what Eliot once had been." If Eliot were to have a lasting place in English poetry, Vendler said, it would "have to be on the basis of the poems written before 1930."[6] Even those poems, she added, might to future readers seem no more than second-rate.

Nor was Vendler alone in her reassessment of Eliot's reputation. Many critics in the years following his death have had little positive to say about his work. In 1999, for example, one critic wrote, "It is difficult to say what is more remarkable: the potency of Eliot's influence at its peak or the suddenness of its eclipse."[7] Perhaps Eliot would have consoled himself by reflecting on a remark he had made in 1933: "No honest poet can ever feel quite sure of the permanent value of what he has written: he may have wasted his time and messed up his life for nothing."[8]

As the twentieth century drew to a close, however, Vendler found herself defending Eliot's reputation as "the most celebrated English-language poet of the century."[9] In a special edition of *Time* magazine, Eliot was selected as one of the hundred most influential artists and entertainers of the century, and Vendler made the case to justify that choice. Eliot's verse, she wrote, at a time when other poets were satisfied with "vague appeals to nature and to God," had succeeded in "reclaim[ing] for American poetry a terrain of close observation and complex intelligence that had seemed lost."[10]

At about the same time, other, younger critics also began to read Eliot's work from new points of view and to find much of value in it. Eliot himself had claimed as early as 1919 that writers need to be constantly reevaluated. For that reason, young readers today have a real role to play in helping determine Eliot's legacy. If they find that Eliot's words are as meaningful for them in the 21st century as they were to earlier generations of readers, they can demonstrate that "This is no longer the age of Eliot, but Eliot is none the less a poet for our time."[11]

READING ELIOT'S POEMS

Part of the problem for young readers approaching Eliot's poems today is their place in the school curriculum. When readers of *The Waste Land* or "The Love Song of J. Alfred Prufrock" know they are going to be tested on their reading, it may be hard for them to respond naturally to the poems. They are likely to believe that the poems are puzzles to be worked out. As Ted Kooser, the thirteenth poet laureate of the United States, said in a 2006 radio interview, poems are not like a calculus problem, with a single correct solution. Kooser encouraged readers to engage personally with a poem in order to find out what it communicates to them as individuals.

Young readers of Eliot would do well to heed Kooser's advice. While a student guide to T. S. Eliot can bring certain useful bits of background knowledge to readers' attention, readers must wrestle with poems on their own. Only then can they know just what a poem means to them personally. In 1961 Eliot said, "Good commentaries can be very helpful, but to study even the best commentary on a work of literary art is likely to be a waste of time unless we have first read and been excited by the text commented upon even without understanding it." The following year he wrote, "I want my readers to get their impressions from the words alone and from nothing else."[12] On another occasion he said, "the whole interest of the process is in getting your own meaning out of it."[13]

In a 1929 essay on the Italian poet Dante (1265–1321), one of his favorite writers, Eliot wrote, "genuine poetry

This photo of T. S. Eliot was taken in the poet's London office in January 1956.

can communicate before it is understood."[14] In a 1950 lecture called "What Dante Means to Me," Eliot explained his growing appreciation for Dante as a college student. Even when he could not make total sense of Dante's words, he would enjoy reciting them to himself in bed or on a train trip. In the same way, according to the director of Eliot's plays, Eliot's "writing must be absorbed before it can be understood."[15]

Eliot also believed that readers were entitled to reach conclusions about poems that had never occurred to the poets who wrote them. In 1931 he wrote the literary critic I. A. Richards (1893–1979) that "a good poem should have a potentiality of evoking feelings and associations in the reader of which the author is wholly ignorant. I am rather inclined to believe, for myself, that my best poems are possibly those which evoke the greatest number and variety of interpretations surprising to myself."[16] Based on his own experience reading the work of others, he also understood that readers should expect their interpretations of a given work to change over time. In his essay "To Criticize the Critic," he wrote, "what has best responded to my need in middle and later age is different from the nourishment I needed in my youth."[17]

Readers encountering Eliot's poems for the first time may be put off by the realization that they are filled with references to other works of literature about which they know nothing. They should not despair. In the decades since Eliot's poetry was first published, countless words have been written "explaining" the poems. Nonetheless, there is no agreement on what any of his individual poems "means." One of the early reviewers of *The Waste Land*, the American critic Edmund Wilson (1895–1972), wrote:

> It is not necessary to know anything about . . . Mr. Eliot's allusions to feel the force of the intense emotion which the poem is intended to convey. . . . [Eliot's] very images and the sound of the words—even when we do not know precisely why he has chosen them—are charged with a strange poignancy which seems to bring us into the heart of the singer.[18]

So one way for readers to begin to immerse themselves in Eliot's works is to read them aloud, to make themselves aware of the poems' rhythms. Even better would be to listen to Eliot reading his own work.

One of Eliot's literary friends, the English writer Virginia Woolf (1882–1941), remembered Eliot's reading *The Waste Land* aloud: "He sang it & chanted it[,] rhythmed it. It has great beauty & force of phrase: symmetry; & tensity. What connects it together, I'm not so sure. . . . One was left . . . with some strong emotion."[19]

Another strategy for new readers is to pay close attention to the structure of Eliot's poems. *The Waste Land*, for example, is made up of five sections, as is each of Eliot's *Four Quartets*.

ELIOT'S PHRASES AND 21ST-CENTURY EXPERIENCE

In 1945, Eliot wrote that poetry "makes a difference to the speech, to the sensibility, to the lives of all the members of a society, to all the members of the community, to the whole people, whether they read and enjoy poetry or not: even, in fact, whether they know the names of their greatest poets or not."[20] As today's young readers prepare themselves to help determine Eliot's long-term legacy, they will begin to notice how his words continue to be quoted in 21st-century contexts.

Over a random two-month period in a recent year, for example, Eliot's poetry was referred to in three separate articles in *The New York Times*. In pronouncing a sentence of life in prison to Zacarias Moussaoui, the only person to date convicted in a United States court for involvement in the September 11, 2001, hijackings, Judge Leonie Brinkema addressed herself to the thirty-seven-year-old prisoner: "'Mr. Moussaoui, you came here to be a martyr and to die in a great big bang of glory. But to paraphrase the poet T. S. Eliot, instead you will die with a whimper,' she added, referring to the famous poet."[21] The poem to which the judge was referring was Eliot's *The Hollow Men* (1925).

A few weeks later, a review of the Cannes Film Festival referred again to the same poem in a different context—its incorporation into *Southland Tales*, a film aired at the festival: "'Southland Tales' opens with a line from T. S. Eliot's poem 'The Hollow Men' ('This is the way the world ends') and a nuclear bomb exploding above a Fourth of July gathering."[22]

The following month, an article about the end of the school year referred to the famous opening words of *The Waste Land:* "April is the cruellest month."[23] The reporter wrote, "The poet T. S. Eliot once said that April was the cruelest month. How would he have felt as a second grader, stuck in a classroom while a spectacular summer blossomed? Might he have chosen June instead?"[24]

During the same period, the dramatic series *Jericho* had its premiere on American television with an episode whose title—"A Pair of Ragged Claws"—comes from "The Love Song of J. Alfred Prufrock."[25]

As one critic put it, "in giving us words to remember and repeat in contexts of our own . . . he brought the one gift a poet can offer: not 'ideas' but assurance that the way we find ourselves living needn't leave us mute, can indeed be spoken about."[26] It may be too soon to assess the long-term legacy of T. S. Eliot's work, but clearly it still helps us in the 21st century make sense of a multitude of experiences.

THE MARCH HARE

The Roots and Development of T. S. Eliot's Earliest Work

In "Tradition and the Individual Talent" (1919), one of his most famous essays, Eliot wrote, "Honest criticism and sensitive appreciation is directed not upon the poet but upon the poetry."[1] In other words, readers should focus on a poet's work, not on the details of his or her life. In practice, however, Eliot did not always follow his own pronouncement. On a radio broadcast in May 1959, for example, Eliot said of the recently deceased British poet Edwin Muir (1887–1959), "We also understand the poetry better when we know more about the man."[2] Similarly, readers today can deepen their understanding of Eliot the poet, playwright, and critic by learning more about the particulars of his life.

IDENTITY ISSUES

Like all young people, T. S. Eliot spent his early years searching for his personal identity. From boyhood Eliot felt uncertain about his regional identity: A native of St. Louis, Missouri, was he a southerner? Or, as the descendant of an eminent New England family that continued to spend summers on the New England coast, was he a northerner? After all, he finished high school and went to college and university near Boston. As a young adult, searching for poets on whom to model himself and finding none in America, he turned to France for inspiration. Did that make him French in some sense? Later still, by marrying an English woman in 1915 and becoming a British citizen in 1927, he seemed to turn his back on his American roots.

On April 23, 1929—St. George's Day, the English national holiday—Eliot described this confused geographical identity to his friend Herbert Read, a British art historian and poet:

> Some day . . . I want to write an essay about the point of view of an American who wasn't an American, because he was born in the South and went to school in New England as a small boy . . . but who wasn't a southerner in the South because his people were northerners in a border state and looked down on all southerners and Virginians, and who so was never anything anywhere and who therefore felt himself to be more a Frenchman than an American and more an Englishman than a Frenchman and yet felt that the U.S.A. up to a hundred years ago was a family extension. . . .[3]

MISSOURI AND MASSACHUSETTS BOYHOOD

Born on September 26, 1888, Thomas Stearns Eliot was the seventh and last child of businessman Henry Ware Eliot, a principal in the Hydraulic-Press Brick Company in St. Louis, and poet Charlotte Champe Stearns Eliot, who had trained as a teacher. His parents were already both in their mid-forties. Tom, as he was called, had an older brother, Henry, and five older sisters. Ada, his oldest sister, was already nineteen when little Tom was born. In April 1943, on her deathbed, Ada wrote in her last letter to her now famous brother: "When you were a tiny boy, learning to talk, you used to sound the rhythm of sentences without shaping the words—the ups and down of the things you were trying to say. I used to answer you in kind, saying nothing yet conversing with you as we sat side by side on the stairs at 2635 Locust Street. And now you think the rhythm before the words in a new poem!. . . ."[4]

Probably the most important family influence on Tom, however, was neither his parents nor his siblings. Rather, it was his grandfather, the Reverend William Greenleaf Eliot. Grandfather Eliot had studied theology at Harvard University's Divinity School. In 1834 he left his New England home behind and moved to St. Louis. His purpose in doing so was to introduce the Unitarian religion to the American frontier. Although still Christians, Unitarians reject some beliefs that are central to other

In this photograph, a six-year-old T. S. Eliot sits on the porch of a home his family owned in Gloucester, Massachusetts.

Christian denominations. The rejected beliefs include original sin—the conviction that human beings are essentially inclined toward evil, an inclination inherited from Adam as a result of his sin in the Garden of Eden. Unitarians have a more optimistic belief in the essential goodness of human nature. They also reject the concepts of hell and damnation and deny the doctrine of the Trinity—that a single divine being unites the Father, the Son, and the Holy Ghost. Eliot once explained that he had been brought up "outside the Christian Fold," in a religion where "The son and the Holy Ghost were not believed in, certainly; but they were entitled to respect."[5]

Although the reverend died the year before Tom's birth, Eliot later explained how his grandfather's presence continued to pervade the family home even after death: "I was brought up to be very much aware of him: so much so, that as a child I thought of him as still the head of the family—a ruler for whom *in absentia* my grandmother stood as viceregent. The standard of conduct was that which my grandfather had set; our moral judgments, our decisions between duty and self-indulgence, were taken as if, like Moses, he had brought down the tables of the Law and any deviation from which would be sinful."[6] The most important of the laws taught by his grandfather was the need to put the needs of the community and the needs of the Unitarian Church above the wishes of the individual. When Tom was sixteen, his mother's biography of Grandfather Eliot was published. Charlotte Eliot dedicated *William Greenleaf Eliot: Minister, Educator, Philanthropist* to her children, "Lest They Forget."

Tom was introduced to another religious heritage entirely, however, by his nursemaid, Annie Dunne. Eliot later remembered accompanying Annie "to the little Catholic church which then stood on the corner of Locust Street and Jefferson Avenue, when she went to make her devotions."[7]

It was also in Annie Dunne's company that Tom went to his first school, Mrs. Lockwood's, which he attended from about the ages of six to ten. His earliest poem, consisting of four short verses, dates from this period. In it the youthful poet lamented having to return to school each Monday morning. From 1898 to 1905 he attended Smith Academy, one of several educational institutions Grandfather Eliot founded in St. Louis. In his final semester there the *Smith Academy Record* published some of the future poet's work.

Eliot later traced his birth as a poet to a discovery he made while at Smith Academy: "I can recall clearly enough the moment when, at the age of fourteen or so, I happened to pick up a copy of Fitzgerald's *Omar* which was lying about, and the almost overwhelming introduction to a new world of feeling which this poem was the occasion of giving me. It was like a sudden conversion; the world appeared anew, painted with bright, delicious and painful colours."[8] *The Rubaiyat of Omar Khayyam* is the title given to a group of short poems originally by Persian poet Omar Khayyam (1048–1122) and later collected and translated by English writer Edward FitzGerald (1809–1883), as his name is more usually spelled. With their theme of "drink and be merry for tomorrow we die," FitzGerald's verse conveyed a very different morality from Grandfather Eliot's. In his *Lectures to Young Men*, Grandfather Eliot warned his audience to avoid alcohol, which promoted "lust" and the "lewd and lavish act of sin."[9]

Eliot later told an interviewer, "I began . . . under the inspiration of FitzGerald's *Omar Khayyam*, to write a number of very gloomy and atheistical and despairing

T. S. Eliot at age ten in 1898.

quatrains in the same style, which fortunately I suppressed completely—so completely that they don't exist. I never showed them to anybody."[10]

After Tom graduated from Smith Academy in spring 1905, he did a postgraduate year at Milton Academy in the Boston suburb of Milton, Massachusetts. There he became conscious of his Missouri drawl and trained himself to speak like his New England cousins with whom he spent summers at the shore. A Milton Academy education was thought to be the best preparation for admission to Harvard. Along with some of his Milton classmates, Tom entered Harvard in autumn 1906. The university was then headed by a cousin, Charles William Eliot.

HARVARD

Eliot's academic career at Harvard did not begin successfully. His highest grade was a C+ in German. Although destined to be the dominant figure in English literature in the decades to come, Eliot earned a grade of unsatisfactory in English. Only by working diligently was he able to remove himself from academic probation in early 1907.

Thereafter, Eliot's Harvard career flourished. He was able to complete the requirements for an undergraduate degree in only three years, and chose then to stay for a fourth, in which he completed a master's degree in English literature. He developed a close friendship with Conrad Aiken, who shared his love of popular theatre and of poetry. Aiken and Eliot were colleagues at the college's literary magazine, *The Harvard Advocate*, which published ten of Eliot's poems between 1907 and 1910. The tenth of these poems, "Ode," was also published in local newspapers after Eliot read it during the Commencement ceremonies in Sanders Theatre.

In 1907 or 1908 Eliot first came across the work of French poet Charles Baudelaire (1821–1867). Fourteen years later, Eliot introduced into *The Waste Land* Baudelaire's technique of drawing on images from daily city life. At this time, however, Eliot found Baudelaire's work too intimidating. In December 1908, toward the end of the first semester of Eliot's third year at Harvard, he came across a book in the *Advocate's* library that was to have an even greater impact on him than FitzGerald's had earlier. The *Symbolist Movement in Literature*, by English poet and critic Arthur Symons (1865–1945), introduced him to the work of French poets like Jules Laforgue (1860–1887), who were influenced by Baudelaire. Although the precise meaning of Symbolist language might not be clear, the images and metaphors the poets selected aimed to express individual emotional experience. Eliot was so impressed by the quotations from Laforgue in Symons's book that he went directly to Schoenhof's, a foreign language bookstore near Harvard. When the two volumes of Laforgue's complete works that he ordered arrived, he inscribed them "Thomas Eliot 1909."

Toward the end of his life, Eliot explained the influence of Baudelaire and Laforgue on his poetic career:

BAUDELAIRE AND LAFORGUE

From Baudelaire's "The Seven Old Men," translated by William Aggeler, *The Flowers of Evil* (Fresno, Calif.: Academy Library Guild, 1954).

> Teeming, swarming city, city full of dreams,
> Where specters in broad day accost the passer-by!
> Everywhere mysteries flow like the sap in a tree
> Through the narrow canals of the mighty giant. . . .
> A dirty yellow fog inundated all space,
> I was following, steeling my nerves like a hero,
> Arid arguing with my already weary soul,
> A squalid street shaken by the heavy dump-carts.

> (http://fleursdumal.org/poem/221)

From Laforgue's "The Coming of Winter," translated by William Jay Smith, *Selected Writings of Jules Laforgue* (New York: Grove Press, 1956), pp. 91–92.

> Now is the time when rust invades the masses,
> When rust gnaws into the kilometric spleen
> Of telegraph wires on roads where no one passes. . . .
> O flannels, hotwater bottles,
> pharmaceuticals, dreams,
> Curtains parted on balconies along the strand
> Before an ocean of suburban roofs,
> O lamps and engravings, cakes and tea,
> Have you alone remained faithful to me? . . .

I think that from Baudelaire I learned first, a precedent for the poetical possibilities, never developed by any poet writing in my own language, the more sordid aspects of the modern metropolis. . . . From him, as from Laforgue, I learned that the sort of material that I had, the sort of experience that an adolescent had had, in an industrial city in America, could be the material for poetry, and that the source of new poetry might be found in what had been regarded hitherto as the . . . unpoetic. That, in fact, the business of the poet was to make poetry out of the unexplored resources of the unpoetical; that the poet, in fact, was committed by his profession to turn the unpoetical into poetry.[11]

He also said that Laforgue was "the first to teach me how to speak, to teach me the poetic possibilities of my own idiom of speech."[12] In short, Eliot's discovery of Baudelaire and the Symbolists in 1907–1908 reassured him that he could use language and imagery similar to theirs to invigorate English poetry.

A YEAR IN PARIS

By 1934, Eliot had been editor of his own journal, *The Criterion*, for twelve years. In his "Commentary" in the April issue of that year, he explained what drew him to Paris in 1910–1911: "Younger generations can hardly realize the intellectual desert of England and America during the first decade and more of this century. . . . The predominance of Paris was incontestable."[13] In 1940 he explained further in notes for a lecture that was never delivered: During his last two years at Harvard College, there was "not one older poet writing in America whose writing a younger man could take seriously." It seemed natural to him then to wish to leave "a country in which the status of poetry had fallen still lower than in England."[14] In a piece Eliot wrote for a French journal in 1944, he added, "It wasn't an accident that led me to Paris. For several years, France represented mainly, to my eyes, *la poésie* [poetry]."[15] In 1959 an interviewer asked him, "Did you think at all about becoming a French symbolist poet. . . ?" Eliot answered, "I only did that during the romantic year I spent in Paris after Harvard. I had at that time the idea of giving up English and trying to settle down and scrape along in Paris and gradually write French."[16]

What seemed self-evident to Eliot, however, seemed eccentric to his parents. It was bad enough that their youngest child dreamed of a career as a writer, unlike his cousins who chose more respectable careers in health, the Unitarian ministry, and public service. But if he insisted on a literary career, why choose Paris instead of New York? On April 3, 1910, Charlotte Eliot sent a concerned letter to Tom: "I suppose you will know better in June what you want to do next year. . . . I can not bear to think of your being alone in Paris, the very words give me a chill. English speaking countries seem so different from foreign. I do not admire the French nation, and have less confidence in individuals of that race than in English."[17]

Eliot did not yield to his mother's wishes, however. In

autumn 1910 he arrived in Paris. He took rooms at a guest house, where he became close friends with a fellow-boarder, Jean Verdenal, a young French medical student. Verdenal introduced Eliot to the conservative French political movement, the Action Française. Led by Charles Maurras, the Action Française was antidemocratic and anti-Semitic. Maurras sought to restore the French monarchy, which he believed was the only institution that might reunite French society. During World War I Verdenal served as a medical officer in the French army. He died in battle in the Dardanelles, the strait between European and Asian Turkey. Eliot dedicated his first book, *Prufrock and Other Observations* (1917), "For Jean Verdenal, 1889–1915."

Studies occupied much of Eliot's time in Paris. He took private French lessons from a French novelist, attended lectures at the Sorbonne (part of the University of Paris), and went to weekly talks given at the Collège de France by philosopher Henri Bergson. Eliot was particularly impressed by Bergson's novel ideas about time. Bergson contrasted "duration," or lived time, to the scientists' time, which is measured by a clock. Eliot's own thoughts about time would later become a major theme in *Four Quartets*.

In April 1911 Eliot made his first visit to London. That summer Conrad Aiken visited Eliot in Paris. Over a soft drink at an outdoor cafe, Eliot confided in him his decision to return to Harvard to study philosophy. He was clearly not ready to give up his dreams of writing poetry,

It is estimated that Eliot was in his early twenties at the time this unattributed photo was taken.

however. Before traveling back to the States in September, Eliot visited Munich and Northern Italy. During this excursion he completed the final version of "The Love Song of J. Alfred Prufrock," which he had begun writing the previous year.

GRADUATE WORK IN PHILOSOPHY

Eliot spent the next three school years as a Harvard graduate student in philosophy. In order to study Indian philosophy, he learned Sanskrit and Pali, the language of Buddhist scriptures. These studies would later influence *The Waste Land* and *Four Quartets*. Eliot's course work also included topics from the new field of psychology, then taught in Harvard's philosophy department. His reading included studies of hysteria, of primitive religions, and of mysticism.

In 1912, Eliot was appointed an Assistant in Philosophy, and in 1913, he became president of the University Philosophical Club. The following year he bought *Appearance and Reality*, the chief work of British philosopher F. H. Bradley (1846–1924). The book presented Bradley's idea that personal experience differs from reality. While personal experience is marked by many contradictions, reality is a harmonious whole, or absolute. After reading Bradley's book, Eliot decided to write his doctoral thesis on Bradley's ideas on the origin and limits of human knowledge.

During graduate school Eliot also forged two friendships that would prove important in his later life. By 1912 he had been introduced to Emily Hale by his cousin Eleanor Hinkley, who held amateur theatrical events at her family's home near Harvard. Three years younger than Eliot, Hale was the daughter of a Unitarian minister. In his sixties, Eliot wrote that in summer 1914 he told Hale that he was in love with her. He interpreted her reaction as proof that she did not return his affection. Hale would play a major role in Eliot's life over the decades to come.

In March 1914 Eliot learned that he had won a Sheldon Traveling Fellowship in philosophy. As a Sheldon Fellow he planned to study at Oxford during 1914–1915 with Bradley's student Harold Joachim. Shortly before he was appointed Sheldon Fellow, Eliot met Bertrand Russell (1872–1970), one of the greatest twentieth-century philosophers. Russell, a member of an old and noble British family, had come to Harvard as a visiting professor. Eliot took a tutorial in logic from Russell, who was considered the greatest logician since the ancient Greek philosopher Aristotle. The student-teacher relationship would become much closer and much more complicated when Eliot and Russell met again in England in 1915.

EARLY POEMS

In the summer of 1910 Eliot visited the Old Corner Bookstore in Gloucester, Massachusetts, where his family had a summer home. There he bought a notebook on which he inscribed a title, which he later crossed out: *Inventions of the March Hare*. Into this notebook he copied poems he had been writing since November 1909, excluding most of those published in *The Harvard Advocate*. He used the notebook during his year in Paris, during his graduate school years at Harvard, and for three years after his arrival in England in 1914. By dubbing the author of the poems collected in the notebook "the March Hare," Eliot compared himself to a character from the tea party scene in Lewis Carroll's *Alice's Adventures in Wonderland*. The notebook and its contents were lost for many years. After they were located in the New York Public Library in the late 1960s, they were published in 1996.

Made available to the general public for the first time were forty poems by young Eliot that had until 1996 been known only to scholars. These include a small group of sexually provocative poems. The volume also includes early versions of nineteen poems that later appeared in Eliot's first four published books, which came out in 1917, 1919, and 1920. These include satires on Boston society and scenes of city life. One of the exciting discoveries was Eliot's early drafts of lines that in later, more polished form would become famous. Among the best known lines from "The Love Song of J. Alfred Prufrock," for example, are "In the room the women come and go/Talking of Michelangelo."[18] An earlier, less successful version of these lines appears in an *Inventions of the March Hare* poem, "Afternoon": "The ladies who are interested in Assyrian Art/Gather in the Hall of the British Museum."[19]

(The French poet Jules Laforgue, whom Eliot admired so much, had previously written, "In the room the women come and go/Talking of the masters of the Sienne school."[20])

According to one reviewer:

> *Inventions of the March Hare* finally allows us to watch the steady evolution of artistic genius. From the beginning Eliot's language displayed authority far beyond his years. How many twenty-three-year-old graduate students write with such dark and mature sonority?. . . *Inventions of the March Hare* expands, deepens, and qualifies our knowledge of the central figure in English-language Modernism. For readers of Eliot, it is an indispensable book.[21]

When Eliot embarked on his traveling fellowship, no one had yet called the kind of poetry his notebook contained "modernist." No one but a small group of friends had even seen the poems in *Inventions of the March Hare*. Within a year, however, the situation would change. Eliot would make the acquaintance of another American in England who—for better and for worse—would permanently alter his life.

MOMENTOUS CHANGES

Examining "Prufrock"

Eliot planned to begin his Sheldon Fellowship with a summer course for foreign students in Marburg, Germany. On August 1, 1914, however, shortly after his arrival in Germany, what would later be called World War I broke out. The course, which had been scheduled to begin on August 3, was canceled. As soon as he could, Eliot departed for England, where he arrived on August 21. The semester at Oxford would not start until October, and Eliot spent the weeks in between in London.

LONDON VS. OXFORD

When Eliot arrived in London, Conrad Aiken, his Harvard friend, had recently left after spending the summer there. While in London Aiken had tried to interest a number of people in Eliot's poems as well as his own. Aiken later recalled giving Harold Monro, editor of *Poetry & Drama*, the manuscript of "The Love Song of J. Alfred Prufrock" to read. After reading it, Monro proclaimed that the author was "absolutely insane" and "practically threw" Eliot's poem back at Aiken. At that point Aiken went to visit Ezra

Pound (1885–1972), an American-born poet who had been living in England since 1908. Pound had recently become the "foreign correspondent" for *Poetry*, a magazine founded by Harriet Monroe in Chicago. When Pound asked Aiken if he could recommend any "genuinely modern" poet, Aiken mentioned Eliot as a "guy at Harvard doing funny stuff."[1]

At Aiken's suggestion, Eliot went to visit Pound on September 22, 1914, in what Eliot called "his little triangular sitting room in Kensington," a neighborhood in southwest London.[2] As he later recalled, "my meeting with Ezra Pound changed my life. He was enthusiastic about my poems, and gave me such praise and encouragement as I had long since ceased to hope for."[3] After reading "Prufrock," Pound wrote to Monroe, ". . . Eliot . . . has sent in the best poem I have yet had or seen from an American. PRAY GOD IT BE NOT A SINGLE AND UNIQUE SUCCESS. He has taken it back to get it ready for the press and you shall have it in a few days."[4]

Pound's efforts on Eliot's behalf did not succeed immediately, but in June 1915, Eliot received payment of eight guineas—worth about $410.00 at the time—when "Prufrock" appeared in *Poetry*. Without Eliot's knowledge, Pound also helped pay the publication costs of Eliot's first book, *Prufrock and Other Observations*, which appeared in 1917. He also arranged for Eliot to review books for different journals as a way of eking out a living.

Pound was not the only person to advance Eliot's interests at the outset of his career. In October 1914, just

A photo wall in the Grolier Poetry Bookshop in Harvard Square in Cambridge, Massachusetts, holds photographs of several significant poets. Here, Eliot is at the upper right while Ezra Pound is on the right in the photo below it.

as Eliot was about to settle into his semester at Oxford, he ran into Bertrand Russell on a street in London. At Harvard the previous spring, Russell had been impressed by Eliot, then a student in Russell's tutorial on logic. Russell now arranged for Eliot to write reviews for philosophy journals. He also introduced him to a group of people different from those in Pound's avant-garde circle. As a member of the English nobility, Russell was able to get Eliot invitations to upper-class homes.

Eliot's initial reaction to Oxford was positive. On October 14, 1914, he wrote a friend who had been at *The Harvard Advocate* with him and Aiken, "I have begun to entertain the highest respect for English methods of teaching. . . . I would give a great deal to have done the regular undergraduate course here." While the war had left Oxford "a quiet and deserted place," he expected it would be "a better place to work in. At any rate, I find it exceedingly comfortable and delightful—and very 'foreign.'"[5]

By December 31, 1914, however, Eliot was disillusioned with Oxford. He wrote Aiken, "Oxford is all very well, but I come back to London with great relief. I like London, now. In Oxford I have the feeling that I am not quite alive—that my body is walking about with a bit of my brain inside it, and nothing else. . . . Oxford is very pretty, but I don't like to be dead."[6] The theme of death in life was one that would haunt Eliot's poetry for years.

When Eliot learned in February 1915 that Harvard had recommended his Sheldon Fellowship be extended for a second year, he wrote Aiken expressing his lack of enthusiasm either for staying at Oxford or for returning to Harvard. "The great need is to know one's own mind, and I don't know that."[7]

Shortly after writing that letter, however, he met a young woman, and the course of Eliot's life changed dramatically.

A DOOMED MARRIAGE

In an April 1915 letter to his cousin Eleanor, Eliot wrote that a new woman had entered his life. She was a "very good" dancer, "quite different from anything I have known at home or here," and "charmingly sophisticated . . . without being hardened."[8] Scofield Thayer, a friend from both Milton Academy and Harvard, was responsible for introducing Eliot to Vivienne Haigh-Wood, a close friend of his sister, Lucy. (Vivienne also spelled her name "Vivien," and both spellings are used in this book.) The daughter of a successful English artist, Vivienne had artistic abilities herself. A few months older than Eliot, like him she had recently been involved with someone else.

On June 26, 1915, only months after meeting, Vivienne and Eliot were married. Lucy Thayer and an aunt of Vivienne's were the only two wedding guests. Neither bride nor groom had alerted their parents to their life-altering decision. Eliot was soon to discover that his bride, who was diagnosed with tuberculosis of the bones in infancy, was not a well woman. She was prone to physical ailments, like migraine headaches, and also to mental distress, including panic attacks. Ezra Pound, who originally encouraged the marriage, ended up dismissing Vivienne as "an invalid always cracking up, & needing doctors, incapable of earning anything."[9]

Eliot seems to have married Vivienne as an excuse to abandon the career path of a professor of philosophy that his parents expected him to follow. In a 1946 letter, Eliot described how he had married "the wrong woman" to escape from "a maddening feeling of failure and inferiority" caused by "trying to make myself into a philosopher and future professor of philosophy."[10] In the 1960s, he expanded on the topic:

> To explain my sudden marriage to Vivienne Haigh-Wood would require a good many words, and yet the explanation would probably remain unintelligible. . . . I was very immature for my age, very timid, very inexperienced. And I had a gnawing doubt, which I could not altogether conceal from myself, about my choice of a profession—that of a university teacher of philosophy . . . my heart was not in the study, nor had I any confidence in my ability to distinguish myself in this profession. I must still have yearned to write poetry. . . . I think that all I wanted of Vivienne was a flirtation or a mild affair: I was too unpractised to achieve either with anybody. I believe that I came to persuade myself that I was in love with her simply because I wanted to burn my boats and commit myself to staying in England. And she persuaded herself (. . . under the influence of Pound) that she would save the poet by keeping him in England.[11]

Bertrand Russell met Vivienne for the first time soon after the wedding. In a letter to his close friend Lady Ottoline Morrell, Russell described his reaction to the couple:

> Friday evg. I dined with my Harvard pupil, [T. S.] Eliot, and his bride. I expected her to be terrible, from his mysteriousness; but she was not so bad. She is light, a little vulgar, adventurous, full of life— an artist I think he said, but I should have thought

her an actress. . . . I think she will soon be tired of him. She refuses to go to America to see his people, for fear of submarines. He is ashamed of his marriage, and very grateful if one is kind to her.[12]

Unfortunately, Russell was more than kind to her. Convincing himself that he loved Eliot "as if he were my son," and that he was bent only on "getting things more right between them,"[13] Russell soon began a romantic relationship with Vivienne. He made space for the struggling couple in his apartment, and helped the Eliots out financially, but did more to damage the marriage than to improve it. For years Russell denied that his behavior was improper in any way, but Eliot and others knew better. Writer Evelyn Waugh, for example, wrote in his diary that Vivienne eventually went mad as a result of "her seduction and desertion by Bertrand Russell."[14]

Russell kept Vivienne company while Eliot traveled back to the States to try to convince his parents that his course of action was the right one. His parents were not persuaded, however. They had been offended by a letter from Ezra Pound defending Eliot's choice of a literary life in London and asking Eliot's father to subsidize his son for the next couple of years until he could "get decently started."[15] They extracted a promise from Eliot that he would complete his work on his Ph.D. thesis. In early 1916 Eliot sent a copy of his completed thesis to Harvard. The department of philosophy accepted it as "the work of an expert,"[16] and Eliot made plans to return to the States for the required oral exam. In the end, perhaps put off by the danger of sailing during the war or by lack of funds, Eliot did not make the trip. He never received his Ph.D., though his thesis was eventually published in 1964.

Eliot's father died in 1919 without ever having met the woman who, in his view, ruined his son's life. Charlotte Eliot did not meet her daughter-in-law until the summer of 1921, when she traveled to England with one of her daughters and with her older son. The Eliots did not turn their backs on their youngest son and his wife. By the terms of Henry Ware Eliot's will, however, whatever money Tom would inherit after his father's death would not become Vivienne's if she should outlive him.

MAKING A LIVING

When Eliot married, he noted on the official document that he was "of no occupation." Once he became a married man, however, he had to figure out how to support himself and his wife. His father's financial help would not suffice to enable Eliot to devote himself to poetry. For nearly two years after his marriage, Eliot had to work very hard indeed to earn a meager living. The stress affected his physical and mental health, too. During the periods when Vivienne was in reasonable health, often he was not.

Eliot tried his hand at teaching at two different grammar schools from autumn 1915 through the end of 1916. The experiment was unsuccessful, as he wrote his brother: ". . . I find that I am losing in every way. I have not time to pursue my literary connections, and overwork is telling on the quality of my production."[17] More successful were the courses he offered to adult working-class people from 1916 to 1918. All the work Eliot invested in preparing these courses in English and French literature paid off. Eliot's poetry would be enriched by the references to the literature he taught, and his literary criticism was shaped by the opinions he reached as he developed the material. As his marriage deteriorated, Eliot also took pleasure in the relationship he developed with his students. He wrote his father on March 1, 1917: "One of the class told me that I was the best literature tutor they had ever had in that class. I enjoy it immensely, and the Monday evening is one of the moments of the week that I look forward to. The class is very keen and very appreciative, and very anxious to learn and to think. These people are the most hopeful sign in England, to me."[18]

In addition to teaching, Eliot also earned money by writing reviews for different magazines. In addition to money, these journalistic assignments offered him "new literary influences," resulting in "different emotions to express."[19] There was no way to know at the time, of course, that these book reviews would help transform Eliot into a famous literary and cultural critic.

What was painfully clear at the time was how hard it was for the Eliots to make ends meet on his income from teaching and writing. In March 1917, thanks to a letter of introduction from a banker friend of Vivienne's family, Eliot was employed by Lloyds Bank. Though in a letter of

March 23 he described his employment there as "a stop-gap,"[20] Eliot remained at the bank until November 1925.

At this stage of his life, Eliot's economic problems seemed a terrible burden to him. Decades later, however, he reflected that the struggle to make a living had been a positive influence:

> I feel quite sure that if I'd started by having inde-pendent means, if I hadn't had to bother about earning a living and could have given all my time to poetry, it would have had a deadening influence on me . . . for me it's been very useful to exercise other activities, such as working in a bank, or publishing. . . . The danger . . . of having nothing else to do is that one might write too much rather than concentrating and perfecting smaller amounts.[21]

PONDERING "PRUFROCK"

On July 2, 1915, Eliot wrote his brother, "You will have heard by this time of the surprising changes in my plans. . . . The only really surprising thing is that I should have had the force to attempt it. . . . I know that you will agree that the responsibility and independent action has been and will be just what I needed."[22] While Eliot was making these momentous changes in his life, the literary charac-ter who launched his career is memorable for his inability to act forcefully and decisively. (Later, Eliot would write a friend that he himself suffered from "an aboulie . . . which has been a life-long affliction."[23] *Aboulie* or *abulia* is a psy-chiatric term for the inability to act decisively.)

> A **dramatic monologue** is a poetic form in which a single character addresses a non-speaking listener, revealing aspects of his or her character and of the dramatic situation.

Growing up in St. Louis, Eliot may have noticed ads for Prufrock-Littau furniture wholesalers. The Christian name the young poet gave to the protagonist of his dramatic monologue suggests a certain prissiness and fussiness.

Careful readers of the poem notice many things, including the following:

1. Prufrock is so fearful of the reaction of others to the image he projects that he is never able to sing his love song, never able to ask the "overwhelming question" to which he refers. He will not "dare/Disturb the universe." He is crippled by "indecisions" and "revisions." His indecisiveness even affects what he eats: He is not sure he dares to eat a peach.

2. The very evening that Prufrock describes is paralyzed and incapable of action, "Like a patient etherised upon a table." Many of the other images in the poem, such as the fog, combine sensuality with drowsiness, resulting in inactivity.

3. Those readers who could understand and identify the Italian epigraph to the poem would connect the paralysis of the evening with the paralyzed self-consciousness of its speaker, Guido da Montefeltro. Prufrock is so worried about being seen through by those he expects to encounter on the visit that he decides not to pay the visit after all.

4. In the middle of the poem, the grammar changes. After Prufrock, suffering from a failure of nerve, has decided not to pay his visit, "Would it have been worth while" takes the place of "there will be time."

5. Even though Shakespeare's Hamlet is often associated with indecision, Prufrock does not feel right comparing himself to any leading figure in a drama, even an indecisive one. He sees himself at best as a minor figure, one whom even the servants mock. He is terrified of embarrassing himself by making a social blunder.

6. The artist Michelangelo painted and sculpted figures that exude great energy and confidence, whereas Prufrock is too timid even to drink fully from the cup of life. Instead he measures out his life in coffee spoons.

When "Prufrock" first appeared in 1915 and then reappeared as the title poem in the 1917 collection *Prufrock and Other Observations*, responses varied. American author and editor Louis Untermeyer (1885–1977) called the poem "the muse in a psychopathic ward drinking the stale dregs of revolt."[24] Publisher Alfred A. Knopf, however, said, "I do not know whether it is great poetry or not. I do know that it is great fun and I like it."[25]

POEMS FROM 1917 TO 1919

To demonstrate to his parents that he had not "made a mess" of his life, "as they are inclined to believe,"[26] Eliot hoped that Knopf would publish an American edition of his poems. Knopf declined, however, because he thought the collection was too small. Eliot worried that he would not be able to write anything to equal "Prufrock" to fatten up his slim collection of poems: "I often feel that 'J. A[lfred]. P[rufrock].' is a swansong, but I never mention the fact because Vivien is so exceedingly anxious that I shall equal it, and would be bitterly disappointed if I do not," he wrote his brother in autumn 1916.[27]

After he began working at the bank, however, Eliot was able to overcome his writer's block. Vivien wrote to her mother-in-law, addressing her as "My dear Mrs. Eliot," on Easter Sunday 1917: "Tom is going on smoothly at the Bank. . . . He writes better, feels better and happier and has better health when he knows that money (however *little*) is *assured*, and coming in regularly."[28]

Oddly enough, he was able to stimulate his poetic abilities again by writing in French. He recalled in 1959, "At that period I thought I'd dried up completely. I hadn't written anything for some time and was rather desperate. I started writing a few things in French and found I *could*. . . . Then I suddenly began writing in English again and lost all desire to go on with French."[29] In 1919 his friends Virginia and Leonard Woolf published 250 copies of a small hand-printed, hand-bound pamphlet containing seven new Eliot poems, including three in French. Many of the new poems contain references to authors and works he had taught his working-class adult students. Eliot was able to use these allusions to convey emotion indirectly.

In February 1920 a British edition of 264 copies of his

work, including his new poems, appeared. Its title, *Ara Vos Prec*, means "Now I pray you" in Provençal, a language once spoken widely in the south of France. Later that month Knopf published a similar collection in the United States under the title *Poems by T. S. Eliot*.

The most significant of the new works is "Gerontion," whose name is Greek for "little old man." Like "Prufrock," "Gerontion" is a dramatic monologue, but its tone is more menacing and more despairing. Gerontion lives in a post-war waste land of "Rocks, moss, stonecrop, iron, merds."[30] In "Gerontion," as in other poems in the new volumes, religion plays an important role. Christ, for example, comes into the world, but "Us he devours."[31] Scattered among the new poems, including "Gerontion," were some disparaging remarks about Jews. These ugly references opened up Eliot to charges of anti-Semitism, which continue to stir much debate today.

By the time these new volumes appeared, Eliot had realized that his marriage was disastrous both for him and for Vivienne. "To her the marriage brought no happiness . . . to me, it brought the state of mind out of which came *The Waste Land*." Furthermore, his "misery with Vivienne" convinced him that he "was still . . . in love with Miss Hale."[32] Significantly, in fall 1923 Eliot sent Emily Hale a copy of *Ara Vos Prec*, inscribed "For Emily Hale with the author's humble compliments, T. S. Eliot, 5. ix. 23."[33]

THE BREAKOUT POEM

The Waste Land (1922)

"I hope to get started on a poem that I have in mind."[1] Eliot wrote these words—his earliest reference to *The Waste Land*—on November 5, 1919, to American lawyer John Quinn. The lawyer and the poet, brought together by Ezra Pound, never met personally. Quinn, however, not only secured the contract for the struggling young poet's first American book but also continued to assist Eliot until his own death in 1924.

WRITING *THE WASTE LAND*

The poem that thirty-one-year-old Eliot had on his mind had actually been developing since he was a graduate student at Harvard. The work went exceedingly slowly. Over a year and a half later Eliot wrote Quinn again, "The chief drawback to my present mode of life is the lack of *continuous* time, not getting more than a few hours together for myself, which breaks the concentration required for turning out a poem of any length. . . . I . . . meanwhile have a long poem in mind and partly on paper which I am wishful to finish."[2]

In addition to his day job at the bank, Eliot was busy preparing for publication a collection of his critical essays. He finally got the manuscript for this book off to his publisher in August 1920, over two months behind schedule. Moving to a new apartment and dealing with family health crises also consumed his time. He did not begin working on the poem in earnest until February 1921. Even then life kept holding up the poem's progress. Vivien's ill health left her "in such incessant and extreme pain" that she "no longer knew reality from delusion."[3] Eliot was her chief caretaker.

A ten-week visit from members of Eliot's family that summer did more than interrupt the writing of the poem. His anxiety before, during, and after the visit led Eliot to a nervous breakdown. He had not seen his family since summer 1915, when he and his parents clashed over the life-altering choices he was making. Now, after his mother, brother, and one of his sisters returned to America in summer 1921, Eliot felt so distraught that he sought medical assistance. On September 1, he wrote a friend, "I am feeling completely exhausted—the departure of my family laid us both out—and have had some splitting headaches."[4] On doctor's orders, he sought and secured a three-month paid leave from the bank. On the eve of his departure, he met with Ezra Pound in London. Pound, who had moved to Paris the previous year, wrote his wife,

"Eliot at last ordered away for 3 months—he seems rejuvinated [*sic*] at prospect."[5]

Eliot began his rest cure in the seaside resort of Margate, about seventy miles east of London. He completed it at a psychiatric facility in Lausanne, Switzerland. Before his family's arrival Eliot had drafted on his old typewriter the first two sections of what became *The Waste Land*, though his working title at the time was *He Do the Police in Different Voices*.[6] After his family's departure he drafted part of the third section on a new typewriter, which his brother Henry had left with him. During the rest cure he completed his rough draft in handwriting. On December 13 he wrote his brother from Lausanne, "I am very much better. . . . I am certainly well enough to be working on a poem!"[7]

En route from England to Switzerland, Eliot had traveled through Paris. There he left some drafts of the ever-lengthening poem with Ezra Pound. On Christmas Eve, Pound wrote these encouraging words to his friend, "MUCH improved. . . . I am wracked by the seven jealousies. . . ." He warned Eliot, however, to keep the poem from growing too long: "The thing now . . . is 19 pages, and let us say the longest poem in the English langwidge [*sic*]. Dont try to bust all records by prolonging it. . . ."[8] Along with his suggestions for improving the poem, Pound enclosed a poem of his own. Calling it "Sage Homme"— French for "male midwife"—Pound's humorous verse describes how "on each Occasion/Ezra performed

A sketch of T. S. Eliot drawn by caricaturist Powys Evans, first published in *The Bookman*, dated December 1930.

the caesarean Operation" that brought forth Eliot's long-awaited offspring.[9]

EDITING *THE WASTE LAND*

Eliot never sought to hide the role that Pound played in shaping the poem the public would later consider his masterpiece. From the time of its first publication in 1922, Eliot had dedicated it to Pound, using the Italian words for "the better craftsman" after his name. The full extent of the changes that Pound made to Eliot's manuscript, however, only became known nearly a full half-century later. To thank John Quinn for taking "such an immense amount of pains on my behalf," Eliot sent him as a present all the manuscripts of the poem. He stressed to Quinn where the value of these manuscripts lay: "In the manuscript of *The Waste Land* which I am sending you, you will see the evidences of [Pound's] work, and I think that his manuscript is worth preserving in its present form solely for the reason that it is the only evidence of the difference which his criticism has made to this poem."[10]

The gift arrived in Quinn's mail in January 1923. After his death the following year, Quinn's sister inherited the manuscripts, which then came into the possession of Quinn's niece after her mother's death. Lost in storage for many years, the drafts of the poem resurfaced in the 1950s. In 1958 they were sold to the New York Public Library, although that fact was not announced publicly for a decade, until the death of the library's curator. In 1971 *The Waste Land: A Facsimile and Transcript of the Original Drafts* was published, edited by Eliot's widow.

With its publication, the full extent of Pound's "operations" on the poem became widely known

FACSIMILE—*the term for an exact copy—is the root from which today's word "fax" derives. A "transcript," by contrast, is a typewritten or printed copy, made by transcribing, or writing down.*

for the first time. Pound reduced the length of the poem from about 1,000 lines to around 435. He suggested cutting Eliot's original opening. Instead of the now-famous words "April is the cruellest month,"[11] the poem originally opened with a first-person account by a jaunty bachelor, of a dissolute evening spent with some similarly carefree chums in contemporary Boston. From the fourth section, "Death by Water," Pound cut eighty-three lines describing a shipwreck off the New England coast, as well as a section describing the decomposition under water of the body of a Jewish victim named Bleistein, the subject of a poem in Eliot's second volume. Pound also crossed out over a page of couplets about a woman named Fresca.

To keep the poem's length under control, Pound also advised Eliot not to include three additional poems at the end. Eliot had been inclined to add these because the English publisher of the book-length version of *The Waste Land* had expressed concern that the poem was too short to justify publication as a separate volume.

In addition to such large-scale cutting of whole passages, Pound also made small-scale changes to particular

> A **couplet** consists of a pair of rhyming verses.

words. For example, Eliot originally had Mr. Eugenides, "the Smyrna merchant" of the third section,[12] speak "abominable" French.[13] Eliot accepted Pound's suggestion and changed the adjective to "demotic,"[14] suggesting that he spoke in "plain, ordinary, everyday language."[15] Similarly, in the second section, where Eliot originally had Lil's husband "coming out of the Transport Corps," Pound substituted the words "got demobbed," the informal words for "was demobilized," or discharged from military service.[16]

As has been noted, "Eliot did not bow to all his friend's revisions."[17] For example, despite Pound's objections in the poem's first part to the hyacinth garden scene and to Saint Mary Woolnoth, Eliot insisted on including them. On the whole, however, Eliot recognized the value of Pound's suggestions. He told an interviewer in 1959, "He was a marvelous critic because he didn't try to turn you into an imitation of himself. He tried to see what you were trying to do."[18]

Similarly, on the whole, reviewers of *The Waste Land: A Facsimile and Transcript of the Original Drafts* marveled at the effectiveness of the collaboration between Eliot and Pound. *The New York Times*, for example, summarized the team effort in this way:

> Watching two of the greatest poets of the century pull a masterpiece out of a grab bag of brilliant material, one has never been so close to the creative process, never on such intimate terms with genius,

or so in touch with literary friendship. . . . The risks of self-expression, the near misses, the sheer effort of creating literature have never been so visible. One reads the final version at the end of the book, after following its perilous evolution, with the joy of hearing a symphony orchestra come together after weeks of rehearsal.[19]

Nonetheless, reviewers and later critics suggested that perhaps Eliot should not have accepted as many of Pound's suggestions as he did. One specific case in point relates to the epigraph, the quotation that precedes the poem and the dedication. Eliot had originally chosen a passage from a fairly recent novel, now considered a literary classic. Pound objected, however, to Eliot's citation of the most famous words from Joseph Conrad's *Heart of Darkness:* "The horror! the horror!" He doubted that "Conrad is weighty enough to stand the citation."[20] Taking Pound's advice, Eliot substituted a passage in Latin and Greek from the *Satyricon,* a fragmentary first-century manuscript that presents a vivid picture of the vices of ancient Rome. Unable to translate the passage, most readers are likely to skip over it. The story of the Sibyl—a goddess trapped in a bottle for the amusement of humans, whose only wish is to die—is doubtless relevant to *The Waste Land.* It is likely, however, that for most readers, the quotation from *The Heart of Darkness* would have offered easier access to the poem.

E P I G R A P H —*A quotation sometimes used at the beginning of a book, chapter, or poem.*

The publication of the facsimile of *The Waste Land* manuscripts also revealed that Pound was not the only editor of Eliot's masterpiece. Vivien also made several valuable suggestions that Eliot adopted. For example, in the description of the working-class married couple, Albert and Lil, in the poem's second section, Eliot had originally used the words, "You want to keep him at home, I suppose."[21] The final version substitutes the line Vivien scribbled on the draft: "What you get married for if you don't want children?"[22]

READING *THE WASTE LAND*

Readers who are struggling with *The Waste Land* for the first time should take heart from the fact that more than eighty years after its initial publication, there is no agreement on many basic issues. Is there a single speaker, for example? Does the poem tell any kind of coherent story? How much attention should the reader pay to the many obscure quotations in English and other languages from which *The Waste Land* sometimes seems to be sewn together? Are the footnotes relevant at all? Does it matter, for example, if one knows anything about "Miss Jessie L. Weston's book on the Grail legend" or about "vegetation ceremonies," as Eliot's notes suggest?[23] Pound, for example, dismissed their value. In 1924 he wrote, "I did not see the notes till 6 or 8 months afterward; and they have not increased my enjoyment of the poem one atom. . . . I have not read Miss Weston's *Ritual to Romance,* and do not at present intend to. As to the citations, I do not think it matters a damn which is from Day, which from Milton, Middleton, Webster, or Augustine. I mean so far as the functioning of the poem is concerned."[24] Even Eliot later regretted including the notes. He had added them "in order to provide a few more pages of printed matter," but the outcome was "that they became the remarkable exposition of bogus scholarship that is still on view today." As a result, "I have sometimes thought of getting rid of these notes; but now they can never be unstuck . . . I regret having sent so many enquirers off on a wild goose chase after Tarot cards and the Holy Grail."[25]

Perhaps the best advice to first-time readers of the poem is to concentrate first on what appears to be going on in each of the poem's five sections, ignoring the notes. The paragraphs that follow aim to focus the readers' attention on some, but certainly not all, ideas worth considering while reading.

I. The Burial of the Dead

The poem begins with a surprising, even shocking, opening lyric. We associate April with spring, and spring with new life, even with love. In the lines and sections that follow, however, April is associated with cruelty, and the love stories that the poem tells are all deeply unsettling. Even first-time readers of *The Waste Land* can see that failed love relationships are a central feature of the poem.

The lyric is followed by five unconnected episodes, all of which are menacing in tone: recollections of a noblewoman named Marie that point out the freedom one feels in the mountains, lines filled with waste land images ("stony rubbish," "a heap of broken images," "the dry stone," "a handful of dust") addressed to the son of man, a scene between lovers in a hyacinth garden that ends in failed communication, a verse paragraph describing a fortune-teller, a final verse paragraph describing the living dead who inhabit London. It may be helpful to think of the five different episodes as scenes in a nightmare. As one critic says, in "our most distressing dreams, . . . [a] dramatic situation emerges, intensifies mysteriously, reverberates with frightening tension and then, just before the situation is clarified, disperses; then a new situation arises that seems comfortingly different but is in fact the same anew."[26]

II. A Game of Chess

This section of the poem focuses on two failed love relationships in the contemporary world. The first, between members of the upper-middle-class, clearly reflects aspects of the relationship between Tom and Vivienne Eliot at the time. Just as the lover in the hyacinth garden "could not/Speak,"[27] here the man says nothing to his partner. He drowns out her neurotic comments by humming inside his head the words of "that Shakespeherian Rag."[28] A rag—short for ragtime—was a style of American popular music, in vogue from about 1899 to 1917. Growing up in St. Louis, Eliot from boyhood enjoyed listening to ragtime performances, which incorporated elements of minstrel shows and African-American banjo

Songbook cover artwork for "That Shakesperian Rag."

music. "That Shakesperian Rag" was an actual song, published in New York in 1912. *The Waste Land* echoes a line in its chorus—"Most in-tel-li-gent, very el-e-gant. . . ."[29]

When Pound read the draft of this section of the poem, he understood that Eliot had based the scene on his tortured marriage to Vivienne, and scrawled in the margin, "photography?"[30] Eliot's friends knew all too well how Vivienne had been known to act on threats such as the one uttered by the wife in the poem: "I shall rush out as I am, and walk the street/With my hair down, so."[31] Two decades after the poem's publication, Eliot pointed out to a friend a spot in London's Trafalgar Square where "Vivienne threw her nightdress out of the window into the street in the middle of the night."[32]

"A Game of Chess" then shifts abruptly into a description by a gossip of the failed working-class marriage of Lil and Albert. It is Eliot's poetic retelling of a story the Eliots' housekeeper, Ellen Kellond, reported. Perhaps Eliot's fond regard for and appreciation of the difficult lives of the working-class students he had recently taught helped shape his sympathetic portrait of Lil. The mother of five children already, with at least one life-threatening childbirth experience, Lil has spent the money Albert gave her not on the set of false teeth he earmarked it for but on pills to abort her current pregnancy. In the waste land, women of all classes suffer.

III. The Fire Sermon

This section expands the poem's examples of loveless sex. Several couples drawn from contemporary city life make brief appearances, including the "nymphs" and "the loitering heirs of City directors"; Sweeney and Mrs. Porter; and Mr. Eugenides, who makes a homosexual advance to the speaker. All are part of what has been called a "catalog of sordid couplings."[33]

The soothsayer Tiresias makes his appearance here. The scene he depicts is of meaningless and mechanical sex between "A small house agent's clerk" and "The typist home at teatime."[34] Toward the end of the section, three women's voices recount unfulfilling sexual encounters in Richmond, Moorgate, and Margate Sands.

By including a reference to a relationship between Queen Elizabeth—the so-called Virgin Queen—and Robert Dudley, Earl of Leicester, "The Fire Sermon" makes clear that loveless waste lands are a feature not only of contemporary life but of human existence over the ages. "A Game of Chess" had already suggested this fact. Among the works of art in the upper-middle-class boudoir is a painting of the rape of Philomel. According to Greek myth, the rapist Tereus tore out Philomel's tongue to keep her from telling her story. Later transformed into a nightingale, Philomel sings "Jug jug"—syllables repeated in both section II and in section III.[35]

In "The Fire Sermon," however, a contrasting way of life also makes a brief appearance. Fishermen gather to "The pleasant whining of a mandoline" in a pub in the financial district of London. The pub looks out on the nearby church of Saint Magnus Martyr, which seems to offer something spiritually untarnished in its "Inexplicable splendour of Ionian white and gold."[36]

IV. Death by Water

When Pound suggested cutting out the bulk of this section from Eliot's draft, Eliot wondered whether he should completely drop Phlebas the Phoenician—the subject of the remaining ten lines. Pound insisted that Phlebas was "ABSOlootly" essential to the poem.[37] After all, part one of the poem already had Madame Sosostris referring to "the drowned Phoenician Sailor," and the silent upper-class husband in part one recalls her words, "Those are pearls that were his eyes."[38] Part three also alludes to death by water by referring to "the king my brother's wreck."[39]

Although there is no agreement about the meaning of this very brief section, Eliot scholar Helen Gardner (1908–1986) described "its suggestion of an ineffable peace, a passage backward through a dream, to a dreamless sleep in which the stain of living is washed away."[40] In other words, for a brief moment the nightmare visions of *The Waste Land* are replaced.

V. What the Thunder Said

The brief peaceful moment of "Death by Water," however, is immediately followed by a reentry into what Gardner calls "a region of nightmare and delirium."[41] In this section the speaker and two companions leave behind the city to travel into a frightening mountainous landscape, where they find an "empty chapel."[42] Behind them the great cities of the ancient and modern world dissolve into "Falling towers."[43]

Eliot later called "What the Thunder Said" "not only the best part" of the poem "but the only part that justifies the whole, at all."[44] Within this section he isolated "30 good lines" he called "the water-dripping song" as his favorite ones.[45] This passage concludes "Drip drop drip drop drop drop drop/But there is no water."[46]

Eliot's training in Indian religion and philosophy at Harvard is apparent in the three mystifying commands of the thunder in lines 396–423. The poem's last lines, however, reflect a mixture of cultural references (including words from the nursery rhyme "London Bridge Is Falling Down") that reflect Eliot's wide reading. The famous line "These fragments I have shored against my ruins" invite many different interpretations. Can anchoring ourselves to the literary tradition of the past somehow save us from the waste land? Or does the fact that most people are ignorant of this literary heritage make such an attempt not only pointless but bordering on madness? Without clarifying anything, the poem concludes with the repetition of the thunder's three words and with the triple repetition of a word that, the notes inform us, means, "The Peace which passeth understanding."[47] Those who could make neither heads nor tails of the poem complained, only partly in jest, that Eliot had simply written a "piece that passeth understanding."[48]

Conrad Aiken, however, found the poem's value not in its notes but in its difficulty: "We reach thus the conclusion that the poem succeeds—as it brilliantly does—by virtue of its incoherence. . . . We could dispense with the French, Italian, Latin, and Hindu phrases—they are irritating. But when our reservations have all been made, we accept *The Waste Land* as one of the most moving and original poems of our time."[49]

ELIOT ON *THE WASTE LAND*

Among the many comments Eliot made about the poem in later years were several regarding his intentions. He told an interviewer in 1959, "I wonder what an 'intention' means! One wants to get something off one's chest. One doesn't know quite what it is that one wants to get off the chest until one's got it off."[50] In an essay written in 1931 he wrote, ". . . when I wrote a poem called *The Waste Land* some of the more approving critics said that I had expressed the 'disillusionment of a generation,' which is nonsense. I may have expressed for them their own illusion of being disillusioned, but that did not form part of my intention."[51] In another essay written in 1927, however, Eliot suggested how the perception might have developed that *The Waste Land* was written to express his generation's pessimism: "The great poet, in writing himself, writes his time."[52]

Eliot also claimed that his choice of a completely new and challenging style for *The Waste Land* was not a conscious attempt to overturn the existing order of poetry.

He told an interviewer, "I don't think good poetry can be produced in a kind of political attempt to overthrow some existing form. I think it just supersedes. People find a way in which they can say something. 'I can't say it that way, what way can I find that will do?' One didn't really *bother* about the existing modes."[53]

ALSO IN 1922

In 1956 Eliot looked back on 1922, when he turned 34, as a watershed year in which he began his "adult life."[54] He pointed not only to the publication of *The Waste Land* in that year but also to his becoming editor of a new journal, *The Criterion*. One of the contributors to *The Criterion*, which Eliot edited until 1939, summarized the journal's importance: "From the beginning it was very distinguished, so that I felt it an honour to contribute. . . . Above all it was the seeing of all European literature as one. . . ."[55]

Vivien's involvement in *The Criterion* also briefly strengthened the unraveling marriage. Not only did she choose the journal's name, but from February 1924 to July 1925 she also contributed to it under several aliases. Eliot was proud of her writing abilities, and she was proud of his ability to carry off his new role despite everything. In an October 1922 letter she wrote: ". . . *The Criterion* . . . seems to me an achievement, by a man who has only his evenings, tired out by eight hours in the City, and who fills hot water bottles, and makes invalid food for his wretchedly unhealthy wife, in between writing."[56]

Editing *The Criterion* bolstered Eliot's self-confidence. Novelist Virginia Woolf recorded in her diary how when Eliot told her he was "starting a magazine," he surprised her by becoming, suddenly, "supple as an eel . . . positively familiar & jocular & friendly."[57]

As 1922 drew to its end Eliot also indicated that one chapter of his life was drawing to a close while another was opening. In a letter of November 15, he wrote, "As for *The Waste Land*, that is a thing of the past so far as I am concerned and I am now feeling toward a new form and style."[58] Just what new form and style his literature—and his life—would take was not yet apparent.

NEW
IDENTITIES

The Hollow Men and *Ash-Wednesday*

I f in some respects things were looking up for Eliot in the early 1920s, it did not take long for his world to fall apart. By July 1922 Vivien was writing to a friend, "You know I am ill and an endless drag on him."[1] He was finding his job at the bank more and more oppressive. His dissatisfaction with work and unhappiness at home led to Bel Esprit, a scheme organized by Pound, to liberate Eliot from his nine-to-five routine and make it possible for him to write full-time. Eliot eventually put a stop to these efforts to raise, through subscriptions, enough private money to subsidize his writing career. Should anything befall him, Eliot knew, Bel Esprit would not provide for Vivien. He wrote Pound in November 1922:

> If I had only myself to consider, I should not bother about guarantees for a moment: I could always earn my own living. But I am responsible toward [Vivien] in more than the ordinary way. I have made a great many mistakes, which are largely the cause of her present catastrophic state of health, and also it must be remembered that she kept me from returning to America where I should have become a professor and probably never written another line of poetry, so that in that respect she should be endowed. . . . In the

71

bank, I am assured £500 a year and perhaps more, and in case of death a widow's pension increasing according to the size of salary.[2]

The publication of *The Waste Land* in the United States and in England in 1922—without notes in *The Criterion* and in the American journal *Dial*, and with notes in book form—brought Eliot fame but not contentment. In 1923 Vivien nearly died. The responsibility of caring for her, on top of the demands of work at the bank and running a journal, left him drained. He wrote John Quinn, "I am worn out, I cannot go on."[3]

FASHIONING A NEW LIFE

In 1923 he seemed to be taking steps toward a breakdown or toward a new life. He rented an apartment where he could work undisturbed by Vivien. Occasionally he spent the night there. His friends noticed signs of some strange behavior. For example, he called himself "Captain Eliot" and wore makeup occasionally. In 1923 he also met and became friends with William Force Stead, an American former diplomat who had been ordained in the Anglican Church (also known as the Church of England). Stead introduced him to the writings of significant Anglican writers and preachers of the seventeenth century.

By 1925 Eliot was ready to turn a corner. With Stead's guidance, he began a journey toward a new religious commitment. He also changed his job, entered a new stage of his career as a poet, and started to imagine a life without

Vivien. In her diary entry for April 29, 1925, Virginia Woolf wrote about her friend Tom: "He has seen his whole life afresh, seen his relations to the world, & to Vivien in particular."[4]

A NEW CAREER, A NEW POETIC FOCUS

In November 1925 Eliot left Lloyds Bank for a position as director of a publishing firm, Faber & Gwyer. (In 1929 the firm's name was changed to Faber & Faber.) According to Frank Morley, one of Eliot's codirectors at the firm, Eliot was originally hired not for his literary insights but for his business experience. Nonetheless, over time he became increasingly involved with editorial matters. One of his early editorial decisions was to arrange the publication of his mother's dramatic poem about the Italian religious reformer Girolamo Savonarola (1452–1498). Charlotte Eliot's poem, with an introduction by Eliot, appeared in 1926 in an edition of 300 copies.

Eventually Eliot became responsible for the firm's poetry list. In this capacity he helped shape the next generation of poets writing in English. For example, W. H. Auden (1907–1973) first published in Eliot's *Criterion* and became a Faber poet in 1930. Auden would go on to win the Pulitzer Prize in 1948 for his book-length poem *The Age of Anxiety*.

Other writers whose careers Eliot helped launch include Stephen Spender, Robert Lowell, Ted Hughes, and

Sylvia Plath. Stephen Spender later remembered that "Eliot encouraged, talked with, wrote to young poets." He contrasted Eliot's nurturing of young writers with the tendency of the editors of the journal *Scrutiny*. Although *Scrutiny* "also maintained and presented high standards," its editors often went out of their way "with young writers to destroy a reputation before it was made."[5]

In a 1953 interview, Eliot reflected on his successful career change: "I have enjoyed being a publisher, . . . and I doubt if I could have found any other occupation to suit my needs so well." He also implied that, suffer at the bank as he did, it was perhaps just as well that he had not worked as an editor from the outset: ". . . I became a publisher only at the age of 39, when my mind, my poetic personality, was more or less formed. I'm not so sure it's a good thing for a young man at the outset of his career, if he wants to write. It's too close to literature—it may blunt your sensibility."[6]

Eliot's memory was slightly faulty in that interview. He was not yet thirty-seven when he joined Faber, and his poetic personality was still forming. The two central poems of this crisis period of his life—*The Hollow Men* and *Ash-Wednesday*—support this assertion. Although his method of composing these poems resembles his method for *The Waste Land*, in style and tone they are quite different. Like *The Waste Land*, both new works were woven together out of separate pieces. Eliot recalled in 1959, "That's one way in which my mind does seem to have worked throughout the years poetically—doing things separately and then seeing the possibility of fusing them together, altering them, and making a kind of whole of them."[7] In addition to fashioning these poems from separate units, Eliot also made use in *The Hollow Men* of a reference that Pound had edited out of *The Waste Land.* Pound had dismissed for the earlier poem Eliot's original epigraph from Joseph Conrad's *Heart of Darkness.* One of the epigraphs Eliot used for *The Hollow Men* is a quotation from that book: "Mistah Kurtz—he dead."[8] In Conrad's novel, Kurtz is the character whose deathbed words were "The horror, the horror," the epigraph Eliot had originally selected to introduce *The Waste Land.*

The Hollow Men and *Ash-Wednesday* convey Eliot's movement toward a new religious commitment. Both poems contain dreams, but they are not as menacing as the nightmares of *The Waste Land.* In *The Hollow Men,* as in *The Waste Land,* a nursery rhyme is used in an unsettling way. Toward the end of the earlier poem, "London Bridge is falling down falling down falling down" suggests the decline and fall for which yet another great metropolis is destined.[9] Toward the end of *The Hollow Men,* the children's song "Here we go round the prickly pear" appears, introducing the speaker's attempt to choose between "the idea" and "the reality," "the motion" and "the act," "the conception" and "the creation," "the emotion" and "the response," "the desire" and "the spasm," "the potency" and "the existence," "the essence" and "the descent." In a sense, we seem to be back in the world of Prufrock, who suffered from paralysis of the will. The poem's speaker is not quite able to complete his religious affirmations. The poem ends with another nursery rhyme, this one Eliot's own creation: "This is the way the world ends/Not with a bang but a whimper."[10] Although these lines are often read as an anguished cry of despair, Eliot scholar Helen Gardner is not so sure. These lines can also be read "as the first sign of the new theme of rebirth. The whimper with which the poem closes may be that first faint querulous sound which tells us that a child is born, and is alive."[11]

Gardner describes Eliot's *Ash-Wednesday* as "the most obscure of Mr Eliot's poems, and the most at the mercy of the temperament and beliefs of the individual reader."[12] The poem expresses the speaker's continued struggle between the worldly life and the spiritual one, but it ends not in psychological torment but in these heartfelt prayers: "Teach us to care and not to care/Teach us to sit still/. . . Our Peace in His will. . . /And let my cry come unto Thee."[13]

When *Ash-Wednesday* was first published in 1930, Eliot included a dedication "To My Wife." In editions published following his separation from Vivien, he omitted the dedication. Perhaps Eliot hoped to convey through lines from the poem his deepest apologies to Vivien for the role he had played in their tortured life together: "Let these words answer/For what is done, not to be done again/May the judgement not be too heavy upon us."[14]

A NEW RELIGION, A NEW NATIONALITY

At the time of its initial publication in 1925, most people read *The Hollow Men* as a logical sequel to the despair of *The Waste Land*. Even Eliot's brother, with whom he was in close touch, did not imagine what was coming. When Eliot fell to his knees before Michelangelo's *Pietà* in 1926, Henry and his wife, who were traveling with him, were astonished. Only after Eliot officially converted to Anglicanism the following year was it clear that *The Hollow Men* marked a step in his personal religious struggle. By the time *Ash-Wednesday* appeared in 1930, his new religious identity was confirmed.

Eliot had been dissatisfied with his family's Unitarianism for many years. He had been raised to believe that "if one was thrifty, enterprising, intelligent, practical and prudent in not violating social conventions, one ought to have a happy and 'successful' life. Failure was due to some weakness or perversity peculiar to the individual; but the decent man need have no nightmares."[15] Clearly nothing to date had succeeded in warding off Eliot's nightmares. The religious struggles he had experienced since boyhood ended when, on June 29, 1927, Eliot was baptized into the Church of England by William Force Stead in Finstock Church, Oxfordshire. Since Unitarians do not accept the formula "in the Name of the Father, and of the Son and of the Holy Ghost," the Anglican Church regarded Eliot as unbaptized. The day

77

after his baptism, Eliot was confirmed in the Church of England by the Bishop of Oxford. As a committed Anglican, Eliot began to attend daily worship services, served as churchwarden, and went periodically on religious retreats. Following his separation from Vivien, he lived for seven years with churchmen in a presbytery. Religious matters began to dominate his writing.

On November 2, 1927, Eliot became a naturalized British citizen. As his friend Sir Herbert Read later remembered, "I was never conscious that he was in any way less English than myself. From the first he fitted naturally into English clothes and English clubs, into English habits generally. In fact, if anything gave him away it was an Englishness that was a shade too correct to be natural."[16] Eliot was known to joke about his supposed transformation from an American to an Englishman. On the stationery of Faber & Faber, he was identified as being of "U.S.A. origin." In one letter Eliot underlined the phrase, adding on the same line, "and dont forget [sic] it."[17] According to Ezra Pound, Eliot's work also would not let readers forget that at root he was American: "It can't be said that an alteration on Mr. Eliot's passport has altered the essential Americanness of his work."[18]

Eliot was deeply serious, however, when he made an announcement in November 1928. In the introduction to a collection of his politically conservative essays published that month under the title *For Lancelot Andrewes*, Eliot called himself "classicist in literature, royalist in politics, and anglo-catholic in religion."[19] Andrewes was one of the seventeenth-century Anglican divines to whom William Force Stead had introduced him some years earlier.

As a Christian writer, Eliot disappointed some of his modernist friends who hoped he would continue in his earlier style. Although Pound and Eliot maintained a personal connection for the remainder of Eliot's life, Pound believed that Eliot's religion undermined his stylistic abilities. When in 1954 Eliot published "The Cultivation of Christmas Trees,"[20] Pound wrote, "Let us lament the psychosis/Of all those who abandon the Muses for Moses."[21] On February 11, 1928, Virginia Woolf commented on Eliot's conversion in a letter to her sister: "He has become an Anglo-Catholic, believes in God and immortality, and goes to church. . . . A corpse would seem to me more credible than he is."[22]

SEPARATION FROM VIVIEN

Virginia Woolf may not have seen Eliot's conversion coming, but she described his movement toward separating from Vivien with a religious image. In a letter of May 18, 1923, she wrote, "That strange figure Eliot dined here last night. I feel that he has taken the veil, or whatever monks do. He is quite calm again. Mrs. Eliot has almost died at times in the past month. Tom, though infinitely considerate, is also perfectly detached. His cell is, I'm sure, a very lofty one, but a little chilly."[23]

Within a few years of his conversion, more than one

friend of the Eliots realized that Vivien had gone off the deep end and that the marriage had become unbearable. In a letter of October 31, 1930, Conrad Aiken described Vivien's appearance and behavior at lunch one day: She "appeared, shivering, shuddering, a scarecrow of a woman with legs like jackstraws, sallow as to face. She examined me with furtive intensity through the whole meal: flung gobs of food here and there on the floor: . . . and during everything constantly directed at T[om] a cold stream of hatred, as he did (so it seemed to me) toward her."[24] In a November 1930 diary entry, Virginia Woolf noted that Eliot had "a leaden, sinister look about him. But oh—Vivienne! Was there ever such a torture since life began,—to bear her on one's shoulders, biting, wriggling, raving, scratching, unwholesome, powdered, insane. . . . This bag of ferrets is what Tom wears round his neck."[25]

In 1932 Eliot received an offer that he viewed as a way out of his marriage. Since leaving his alma mater as a Sheldon Traveling Fellow in summer 1914, Eliot had not been back to Harvard. Now he was invited to spend the academic year 1932–1933 as Norton professor. Eliot departed for the States that autumn intending never to live with Vivien again. He did not personally inform her of the decision, however. Unaware of her husband's intent, Vivien threw a farewell party for him two days before he sailed to America.

He left the dirty work to others. In February 1933 Eliot wrote his solicitor, asking him to prepare a Deed of Separation. He enclosed a letter breaking the news to

Vivien, which he instructed the solicitor to deliver to her personally. The following month he wrote his friend Ottoline Morrell that he would rather never see Vivien again, since it could do her no good to live with a husband who found her both "morally unpleasant" and physically disgusting.[26]

Vivien never accepted the separation from Eliot. Her behavior grew increasingly bizarre. For several years she stalked him at work, at the theatres where his plays were performed, and at poetry readings. She left the door to her apartment unlocked between 10:30 and 11:00 each evening, in case he should decide to return. One year she sent out Christmas cards "From Mr and Mrs T. S. Eliot." Eventually Vivien came to believe that she was the victim of a plot. Vivien's political behavior also struck some of her former acquaintances as a sign of a mental disorder. In 1934 she joined the British Union of Fascists and enjoyed wearing the uniform of this anti-Semitic party.

In July 1938, while Eliot was away on vacation, Vivien was found wandering the streets of London and was taken into police custody. Vivien's brother, Maurice, wrote Eliot, "V had apparently been wandering about for two nights, afraid to go anywhere. She is full of the most fantastic suspicions. She asked me if it was true that you had been beheaded."[27] Maurice signed papers arranging for Vivien to be institutionalized in a private London asylum. Certified insane, she died there of a heart attack in January 1947.

In the meantime, two women entered Eliot's life. In

1927 Eliot resumed regular correspondence with Emily Hale, the American woman he had fallen in love with many years before at Harvard. In 1938 he began a friendship with Mary Trevelyan, the daughter of an Anglican priest. Both women influenced his work over the next decades, though neither relationship inspired a literary masterpiece rivaling *The Waste Land*.

CAPSTONE OF THE POETRY

Four Quartets

During 1932–1933, his year as Norton Professor at Harvard, Eliot traveled across the United States by train to visit Emily Hale at Scripps College, in Claremont, California, where she was then teaching. Although Hale had never gone to university, she had built on her early love of dramatics—the shared interest that had brought her and Eliot together so many years earlier—to become a teacher of drama at colleges and high schools in the United States. In 1934–1935, Hale took a leave from teaching, spending it in England, where she and Eliot spent much time together. After her return to the States, she continued to visit Eliot in England nearly every summer. In the summer of 1937, Hale accompanied Eliot to Edinburgh, where he received an honorary degree from the university. When they were apart, they corresponded by mail. From 1930 until his second marriage in 1957, Eliot wrote her about a thousand letters. Hale also read drafts of his work and made comments and suggestions on them.

EMILY HALE AND BURNT NORTON

During Hale's leave of absence in England, she and Eliot made an excursion to Burnt Norton, a manor house in the Cotswold Hills of Gloucestershire. The day trip, which included a walk in the garden, inspired Eliot's first long poem since *Ash-Wednesday*. Like *The Waste Land*, the poem was divided into five sections. When *Burnt Norton* appeared as the final poem in Eliot's *Collected Poems 1909–1935*, neither Eliot nor readers of that volume had any reason to associate it with musical compositions nor to think of it as the first in a series of four related poems about time. Already in 1930, however, Eliot had confided in William Force Stead—the man who had baptized him into the Church of England—about his hope to write a spiritual autobiography.

At the time, Eliot was experiencing one of his periodic feelings that "pure, unapplied poetry was in the past for me." Upon his return from the United States in summer 1933 he had begun writing dramatic poetry for stage performance, but he considered that *"applied* poetry." Then "a curious thing happened. There were lines and fragments that were discarded in the course of the production" from the first act of his play *Murder in the Cathedral*. As Eliot told an interviewer in 1953, the play's producer rejected the lines on the grounds that it was impossible to "'get them over on the stage' . . . and I humbly bowed to his judgment. However, these fragments stayed in my mind, and gradually I saw a poem shaping itself round them: in the end it came out as 'Burnt Norton.'"[1] Those lines include the thought that "What might have been is an abstraction/Remaining a perpetual possibility/Only in a world of speculation." The rejected lines from the play eventually became the opening paragraph of *Burnt Norton*. Eliot also used in *Burnt Norton* a line that had already appeared in *Murder in the Cathedral:* "Human kind cannot bear very much reality."[2]

Burnt Norton can be read as a love poem to Hale, regretting what might have been had Eliot not married Vivien. The first of its five sections speaks of "the passage which we did not take/Towards the door we never opened."[3] The section closes with the reflection that "What might have been and what has been/Point to one end, which is always present."[4] Both the first section and the final section refer to "the hidden laughter/Of children in the foliage,"[5] a lament, perhaps, for the family Hale and Eliot never had.

THE POET IN WARTIME

While Hale was visiting Eliot in Europe in the 1930s, political events in Europe and Asia were leading the world toward war. During that decade Japan, Italy, and Germany—led by dictators—invaded and took over weak countries. The democratic countries did nothing effective to put a halt to this policy of aggressive territorial expansion. When Germany invaded Poland, however, on

September 1, 1939, Britain and France declared war on Germany two days later. Thus began what would become known as World War II. Hale's departure from England in the late summer of 1939 was hastened by the outbreak of the war. Although the couple was separated by the war, Eliot sent her an inscribed copy of each quartet upon publication.

World War II changed Eliot's life in other ways, too. From early July through the end of October 1940, the Germans waged what became known as the Battle of Britain. The German air force, the Luftwaffe, sought to demoralize the inhabitants of Britain by gaining air superiority over the Royal Air Force. The Germans planned to invade England once the RAF was defeated. In July 1940 Eliot wrote a letter to his friends Geoffrey and Doris Tandy, offering to find homes for their daughters in the United States. "I have relatives in America who wish, and others who ought to be made to, take British children," he wrote.[6] In September 1940 the Luftwaffe began to bomb London and other civilian targets. Air raids, called the Blitz, occurred nearly every night for many months. The bombing led Eliot to leave the clergyhouse in London where he had been living. During the war he lived as a paying guest of the mother of poet Hope Mirrlees in her home at Shamley Green, near Richmond in Surrey. The village was within commuting distance of London, and Eliot continued to work Tuesdays through Thursdays at his office at Faber & Faber. He spent those midweek nights at the Hampstead home of the Fabers, which had a reinforced basement shelter. Choosing to play an active role in civil defense, Eliot also served as an air-raid warden. His base was the roof of the company's offices.

Eliot's concern for himself and others during the Blitz extended to Vivien also. When German buzz bombs began to attack London, he tried unsuccessfully to get her moved from Northumberland House, the asylum where she was a patient, into the country.

Even before the war actually broke out, Eliot decided to give up publication of *The Criterion*, which he had been editing since 1922. The last issue of the journal appeared in January 1939. Eliot wrote in "Last Words," his final editorial, that "the immediate future is not bright," and that "the present state of public affairs" had left him in "a depression of spirits" so deep that he could no longer muster "the enthusiasm necessary to make a literary review what it should be."[7]

The growing unease in Europe had begun to influence Eliot's life even earlier in the decade. After the anti-Semitic and anti-Communist Nazi party came to power in Germany in January 1933, many scientists and teachers were stripped of their jobs. Two months later, the Nazis set up the first of many concentration camps, in Dachau, near Munich. Many intellectuals were thrown into the camp. In December 1933, Eliot received a mailing from Horace Kallen, a Jewish-American philosopher whom he had first met at Harvard over twenty years earlier, and with whom he maintained a thirty-year correspondence. The mailing described a new International League for Academic

Freedom, which sought assistance for "the thousands of teachers and men of science in concentration camps."[8] Immediately upon receiving the mailing, Eliot contacted a colleague at Oxford to see what ideas he might have for assisting professors and scientists fleeing Germany. With the help of Kallen, Eliot helped find a position for economist Adolph Löwe. Both before and during the war, Eliot also assisted other Jewish refugees on his own.

Those who defend Eliot against charges of anti-Semitism point, among other things, both to his friendship with Kallen and other Jews and to his actions on behalf of Jewish refugees. A review of a biography of Eliot published in 2006 suggests that "the young Eliot may well have shared the worst prejudices of his time and place . . . only to overcome them as he matured and saw, with horror, where they led."[9] The matter is not so simple, however. In May 1933, Eliot delivered a series of lectures at the University of Virginia. In one of them, he argued that "reasons of race and religion combine to make any large number of free-thinking Jews undesirable."[10] The following spring the lectures appeared in book form, under the title *After Strange Gods*. Eliot later withdrew the book from publication, but the statement remains "one of the most quoted and disdained in modern literary and cultural studies."[11] Also, in September 1943, at a poetry recital in London's Wigmore Hall, Eliot chose to read "Gerontion," with its disturbing anti-Semitic lines. As has been noted, by that time "the British press knew and had reported upon the fate of Jews under Nazi rule," which the world would later call the Holocaust.[12] More than two-thirds of the Jews in Europe were killed in the Holocaust. Eliot insisted over the years, however, that he harbored no anti-Semitic feelings. Clearly, the issue of Eliot's attitude toward Jews is complicated and not easily resolved.

WORLD WAR II AND ELIOT'S LITERARY FOCUS

The war also shifted Eliot's literary focus from drama to poetry. He recalled in 1953:

> Even 'Burnt Norton' might have remained by itself if it hadn't been for the war, because I had become very much absorbed in the problems of writing for the stage and might have gone straight on . . . to another play. The war destroyed that interest for a time: you remember how the conditions of our lives changed, how much we were thrown in on ourselves in the early days? 'East Coker' was the result—and it was only in writing 'East Coker' that I began to see the Quartets as a set of four.[13]

A few years later Eliot clarified how the war influenced his decision to write poetry instead of plays: "In 1939 if there hadn't been a war I would probably have tried to write another play. . . . The form of the *Quartets* fitted in very nicely to the conditions under which I was writing, or could write at all. I could write them in sections and I didn't have to have quite the same continuity;

it didn't matter if a day or two elapsed when I did not write, as they frequently did, while I did war jobs."[14]

As he had done with *Burnt Norton*, Eliot named each of the remaining three poems for a place. Between 1940 and 1942, each poem was published in turn in the *New English Weekly* and subsequently by Faber & Faber. *East Coker*, which was first published in March 1940, is named for the Somerset village that Andrew Eliot, the poet's ancestor, left behind for New England in 1669. Eliot had visited East Coker in 1937. *The Dry Salvages*, first published in February 1941, refers to a group of rocks off the coast of East Gloucester, Massachusetts, where Eliot's family spent the summer months. *Little Gidding*, first published in October 1942, is named for a Huntingdonshire village that Eliot had visited in 1936. During the seventeenth century it had become home to an Anglican religious community. In May 1943 the four poems were published together for the first time under the title *Four Quartets* in the United States. Faber & Faber published the first English edition in autumn 1944.

In a draft of an essay he called "The Three Voices of Poetry," Eliot originally called the last three quartets "patriotic poems." Each of the poems contains references to wartime events. The third section of *East Coker*, for example, is on one level a description of all classes of Londoners descending into the underground stations, which served as air-raid shelters during the Blitz. Similarly, the second part of *Little Gidding* describes the aftermath of a bombing raid. Without specifically intending to become a public poet, Eliot found himself rallying the two English-speaking Allies—Britain and the United States—with the last three poems. Readers terrified by the successes of the German enemy, for example, could take heart from lines in the final section of *East Coker:* "There is only the fight to recover what has been lost/And found and lost again and again: and now, under conditions/That seem unpropitious."[15]

Eliot also helped bolster morale during the war by making twenty-four radio broadcasts. "On Poetry in Wartime" was aired shortly before one of the decisive victories of the war, at El Alamein in the deserts of North Africa. Eliot told his listeners that "the artist who will do the most . . . for his own people, will be the artist great enough, like Shakespeare, to give something precious not only to his own country but to the whole of Europe."[16]

When *Little Gidding* was published in autumn 1942, the Axis powers of Germany, Italy, and Japan had the upper hand. After the war ended with the victory of the Allied forces, readers no longer searched the poems for patriotic reassurance. In the following decades, among the passages in *Four Quartets* that appeared most meaningful to readers both in Eliot's adopted country and elsewhere is one in the second section of *Little Gidding,* describing an encounter with "a familiar compound ghost."[17] Eliot later identified the ghost as a composite of several poets who had influenced him, including the recently deceased Irish poet William Butler Yeats (1865–1939). Those looking for autobiographical references have focused on lines in this passage that appear to express his regret for the waste of his marriage to Vivien: "the awareness/Of things ill done and done to others' harm/Which once you took for exercise of virtue."[18] That acknowledgment allows the speaker to conclude the final section of the poem, and therefore of all four *Quartets*, with the confession of having achieved "A condition of complete simplicity/(Costing not less than everything)."[19]

FOUR QUARTETS AND JOHN HAYWARD

The Waste Land was ushered into the world by one "male midwife," as Ezra Pound had dubbed himself. John Hayward (1905–1965), another Eliot friend and colleague, played a similar role in shaping *Four Quartets*. Hayward, who studied English and modern languages at Cambridge University, moved to London in 1927. A busy and productive man of letters, Hayward had been diagnosed with muscular dystrophy in boyhood and confined to a wheelchair by 1930. Eliot became part of a group of literary figures who met regularly at Hayward's house. Each member of the group had an animal nickname. Hayward, whose words could sting, was dubbed "Tarantula." Eliot was sometimes called "Elephant" and sometimes "Possum."

A series of letters from Eliot to Hayward and from Hayward to Eliot and others in their circle reveal the nature of the collaboration. Letter XII of "Tarantula's Special News Service" was sent to Frank Morley in February 1940. Hayward wrote, "Well, the old master, Tom, polished off his poem more quickly than he expected. . . . I will tell you that I think that this poem—"East Coker"—is prodigiously fine."[20]

Eliot aired his concerns about the poems-in-the-making to Hayward. For example, as he was writing *East Coker*, Eliot wrote Hayward, "It may be quite worthless, because most of it looks to me like an imitation of myself."[21] In July 1942, while Eliot was working on revisions of *Little Gidding*, Hayward explained that Eliot was afraid that "he was simply repeating himself and so running into the risk of producing an elegant parody of the earlier poems in the group."[22]

Eliot also wrote a letter to Hayward expressing his anxiety about and justification for the overall title for the group of four poems: "I am aware of general objections to these musical analogies. . . . But I should like to indicate that these poems are all in a particular set form which I have elaborated, and the word 'quartet' does seem to me to start people on the right tack for understanding them."[23] In addition to listening to Eliot's concerns, Hayward also made helpful suggestions for ways in which Eliot could improve the phrasing and construction of the poems.

Mary Trevelyan, whom Eliot met in 1938, later wrote, "Besides a strong personal affection, [Eliot] depended greatly on John as his literary critic and seldom felt quite easy in his mind about anything he had written unless John approved."[24]

During the war, Hayward voluntarily took on a position he called "Keeper of the Eliot Archive." Eliot began routinely turning over to Hayward groups of manuscripts and typescripts, as well as all printed editions of his work. After the war Eliot and Hayward shared an apartment in London. The living arrangement, and the friendship, came to an abrupt end in January 1957. On January 10, without a word to his roommate, Eliot married his private secretary, Valerie Fletcher, who had been working for him since 1950. Hayward was stunned by Eliot's behavior, and the two saw each other again only twice. Both Eliot and Hayward died in 1965. In his will, Hayward left his collection of the literary manuscripts of T. S. Eliot to King's College, Cambridge.

CAPSTONE OF A CAREER

Eliot was asked in 1959 to share some thoughts about *Four Quartets*. He contrasted the language of the *Quartets* to that of *The Waste Land:* "I see the later *Quartets* as being much simpler and easier to understand than *The Waste Land. . . .* By the time of the *Four Quartets*, I couldn't have written in the style of *The Waste Land*. In *The Waste Land*, I wasn't even bothering whether I understood what I was saying." When the interviewer asked whether "*Four Quartets* are your best work," Eliot answered, "Yes, and I'd like to feel that they get better as they go on. The second is better than the first, the third is better than the second, and the fourth is best of all."[25]

Eliot was not alone in thinking that the *Quartets* were the capstone of his poetic career. In 1949 Helen Gardner called *Four Quartets* "Mr. Eliot's masterpiece . . . the mature achievement of a poet who has had in a long period of experiment effected a modification and an enrichment of the whole English poetic tradition."[26] A number of critics continue to believe that the series of four poems is Eliot's greatest achievement. Others emphatically do not share that view. By 1971 Helen Vendler, who had in 1950 thrilled to catch a glimpse of Eliot at Harvard, disparaged Eliot's last major poem: Eliot's use of verse, she said, "stretched feebler and feebler through the tracts of the 'Quartets.'"[27]

Following the publication of *Little Gidding*, Eliot published only six poems. In a 1963 article called "Reading Eliot Today," the critic Frank Kermode dismissed those poems as "mostly occasional in character and of no great importance."[28] An occasional poem is one intended to mark a particular occasion. An example is Eliot's "To Walter de la Mare," which Eliot wrote "for inclusion in *Tribute to Walter de la Mare* (Faber & Faber Ltd., 1948),"[29] a book presented to the English author of works for both adults and children on the occasion of de la Mare's seventy-fifth birthday.

Eliot was only in his fifties when he wrote the last of the *Quartets*. He was hardly ready to end his career, but for the remaining years of his life he wrote mainly plays and essays.

THE POET AS PLAYWRIGHT

Eliot on the Stage

Many people identify Eliot only as a poet. In fact, however, just as Eliot spent a little over three decades writing poetry—from his student years at Harvard through the early years of World War II—he devoted roughly the same amount of time to writing for the stage. One could even argue that Eliot spent more time thinking about theatrical matters than about poetry. Over the course of his whole career he wrote about the popular stage and about literary drama. And while *The Waste Land* was still only partly on paper, he had begun thinking about writing a play.

FROM *THE WASTE LAND* TO *SWEENEY AGONISTES*

In September 1920 Virginia Woolf recorded in her diary that Eliot "Wants to write a verse play" revolving around Sweeney, one of his poetic creations.[1] Before making his automotive *Waste Land* visit "to Mrs. Porter in the spring,"[2] the sensual, non-intellectual, non-religious Sweeney made his debut in "Sweeney Erect," "Mr. Eliot's

Sunday Morning Service," and "Sweeney Among the Nightingales,"[3] in Eliot's second collection of poems.

While Eliot worked on revisions of *The Waste Land* he was reading the plays of Aristophanes (c. 448–388 B.C.), the greatest ancient Greek writer of comedy. In September 1924 English novelist and playwright Arnold Bennett (1867–1931) wrote in his diary that Eliot "had definitely given up that [*Waste Land*] form of writing, and was now centred on dramatic writing. He wanted to write a drama of modern life (furnished flat sort of people) in a rhythmic prose 'perhaps with certain things in it accentuated by drumbeats.'"[4]

The combination of Sweeney and Aristophanes and drumbeats culminated in the sketches Eliot later called *Sweeney Agonistes: Fragments of an Aristophanic Melodrama.*[5] Confirming Bennett's memory, Eliot set the action in a London flat at a party hosted by two lower-class women. Eliot had been, since boyhood, a fan of popular entertainments such as vaudeville, comic opera, and jazz. The influence of all three is apparent in the play's scenes and songs.

While Eliot may have put the style of *The Waste Land* behind him to write this work, he had not changed mind sets yet. The meaninglessness of life and the sinfulness of humanity dominate the work. Fortune-telling cards figure in the action. Sweeney, the most thoughtful of the characters, is unable to communicate to the other characters his conviction that life amounts to nothing more than "Birth, and copulation, and death."[6]

In 1925 Eliot told Bennett, who had commented on a draft of the play, that he was abandoning the project because of basic problems with it that he could not solve. Eliot never completed the work. The two "fragments" were published first in 1926–1927 in *The New Criterion* (the official title of Eliot's journal for a time). In December 1932 Faber & Faber published the experimental work in book form. The following May, nearing the end of his term as Norton Professor at Harvard, Eliot was present for the world premiere of *Sweeney Agonistes*, at the Experimental Theatre of Vassar College in Poughkeepsie, New York, then a school for women only. In early 1934 the scenes were performed at the Group Theatre in London.

In a 1936 letter, Eliot wrote that of all his work to date he believed *Sweeney Agonistes* was the most original. What readers today often find most tantalizing is Sweeney's preoccupation with the idea that "Any man has to, needs to, wants to/Once in a lifetime, do a girl in."[7] Eliot explained to the mostly female audience at Vassar in May 1933 that he was not the type "to do a girl in."[8] Those aware of the turmoil he was experiencing in his marriage with Vivien, however, might be forgiven for seeing something autobiographical in Sweeney's obsession.

RELIGIOUS DRAMA

In his final lecture at Harvard in spring 1933 Eliot said, "The ideal medium for poetry, to my mind, and the most direct means of social 'usefulness' for poetry, is the theatre."[9] When Eliot returned to England, however, he was absorbed in his own personal drama of completing the separation from Vivien. As he had at other times in his life, he felt his creative springs had run dry.

Nonetheless, that fall, he accepted a commission to write choruses for a dramatic work on behalf of the Church of England. For a long time Eliot had been interested in the role of the chorus in the drama of ancient Greece. The actors in the chorus commented on the main action of the play. He thus began a collaboration with E. Martin Browne that was to endure for a quarter-century. Browne, then a director of religious drama for the Church of England, was organizing a pageant play, to be called *The Rock*. Some years later Eliot recalled his decision to undertake the new project: "The invitation to write the words for this spectacle—the occasion of which was an appeal for funds for church-building in new housing areas—came at a moment when I seemed to myself to have exhausted my meagre poetic gifts, and to have nothing more to say. To be, at such a moment, commissioned to write something which, good or bad, must be delivered by a certain date, may have the effect that vigorous cranking sometimes has upon a motor car when the battery is run down."[10]

The undertaking, which involved twenty-two scene changes, a cast of over three hundred mostly amateur actors, an orchestra of forty, and a choir, clearly recharged Eliot's batteries. The pageant's two-week run in spring 1934 resulted in some excellent reviews, including this encouraging comment in *The New Statesman:* ". . . it is clear that these choruses, the most prolonged effort the poet has given us since *The Waste Land*, are admirably suited for dramatic delivery, and unlike most modern poetic drama, really written to be spoken as well as read. . . . Mr. Eliot shows himself a greater master of theatrical technique than all our professional dramatists put together."[11]

Among the enthusiastic members of the audience of *The Rock* was George Bell, an Anglican bishop who had previously been dean of Canterbury. In 1928 Bell had inaugurated an annual Festival of the Arts at Canterbury, when a play by poet-playwright John Masefield (1878–1967) had been performed at the Canterbury Cathedral. Using the proceeds of Masefield's play, Bell set up a fund to commission new plays for the arts festival, which continues today. In summer 1934 Bell invited Eliot to write a religious poetic drama to be staged for the Canterbury Festival of the Arts. Eliot accepted the commission, stipulating only that Browne should be his play's producer.

The commission also came with one stipulation: that the subject should be related to the history of Canterbury. As Browne noted, "there is no lack of interesting characters" in Canterbury's history, but Eliot nonetheless chose to write about Thomas Becket (c. 1118–1170), who had been the protagonist of the previous three festival productions. Becket was elevated to sainthood in 1173, three years after his assassination by knights of King Henry II, whose efforts to take control of the English church Becket

9, Clarence Gate Gardens,
London N.W.1

26th February, 1922.

Maurice Firuski Esqre.,
   26, Holyoke Street,
     Cambridge, Massachusetts.

Dear Sir,

Your name has been given me by Mr. Conrad Aiken, who has also shown me a volume of poems by Mr. John Freeman, recently published by you, with the appearance of which I was very much pleased.

I have now ready a poem for which that form of publication seems to me the most suitable. I understand that you issue these books in limited editions, and that for the volumes you take for this series you give a sum down in advance royalty.

My poem is of 435 lines; with certain spacings essential to the sense, 475 book lines; furthermore it consists of five parts, which would increase the space necessary; and with title pages, some notes that I propose to add, etc., I guess that it would run to from 28 to 32 pages.

I have had a good offer for the publication of it in a periodical. But it is, I think, much the best poem I have ever written, and I think it would make a much more distinct impression and attract much more attention if published as a book.

If you are interested in this, I should be glad to hear from you what terms you would be prepared to offer for it, at your earliest convenience, as the other offers for it cannot be held in suspence very long.

I am,

yours faithfully,

T. S. Eliot

A letter from Eliot to publisher Maurice Firuski, recommending the publication of *The Waste Land*. Eliot notes that he considers the work "the best poem I have ever written." Later in his career, Eliot would concentrate more on writing drama.

opposed. According to Browne, Eliot's decision to write about Becket rather than looking "for fresh material" might be related to his own fairly recent religious commitment: "Thomas was Eliot's own first name; and Thomas Becket's gift of his life to 'the Law of God above the Law of Man' had been consciously and specifically made by Thomas Eliot a few years before."[12]

Not surprisingly, Eliot gave the best known lines in *Murder in the Cathedral* to Becket. In Part II, Becket tells the poor women of Canterbury who make up the chorus, "Human kind cannot bear very much reality" (a line he also used in *Burnt Norton*). Toward the end of Part I, Becket addresses not only the chorus but also four tempters, who visit him shortly before his Christmas morning sermon. Becket has no trouble rejecting the temptations held out by the first three tempters: worldly pleasures, lasting power as chancellor, and recognition as leader of the barons against the king. The fourth temptation, however, is unexpected, and less easy to overcome. It is "glory after death," with "pilgrims, standing in line/Before the glittering jewelled shrine" of the saint.[13] Ultimately Becket is able to reject the temptation to let himself be assassinated in order to achieve eternal glory as a martyr. In memorable verse Becket says: "The last temptation is the greatest treason:/To do the right deed for the wrong reason."[14]

The play was received so well in Canterbury that it moved to London in autumn 1935 and to New York in January 1938. While critics were generally enthusiastic about Eliot's marriage of verse and drama, in a 1959 interview Eliot himself expressed reservations about his achievement: "... *Murder in the Cathedral* is a period piece and something out of the ordinary. ... It didn't solve any of the problems I was interested in."[15] The response of his friend Ezra Pound was much more damning. After hearing a radio broadcast of the play in January 1936, Pound wrote American publisher James Laughlin (1914–1997): "Waal, I heerd the 'Murder in the Cafedrawl' on the radio lass' night. ... Mzzr Shakzpeer *still* retains his posishun."[16]

Even if Eliot was not fully satisfied with *Murder in the Cathedral*, it became part of his contribution to his adopted country during World War II. With Eliot's permission, E. Martin Browne and the Pilgrim Players "played the emergency version for three years in every setting from cathedral to air-raid shelter and from theatre to village schoolroom."[17]

PLAYS OF CONTEMPORARY LIFE

The unexpected commercial success of *Murder in the Cathedral*—it was even made into a film in 1951—resulted in opportunities for Eliot to write other religious plays. He turned these down, however. According to Browne, "He had always been wary of repeating himself; but in this matter he was motivated by a positive conviction. If the poets of the twentieth century were to find a place in the theatre, it could only be by writing of contemporary life. Verse . . . must be spoken by people living the same life as their audience."[18] During the two decades between 1938 and 1958, Eliot wrote four plays with modern settings and middle-class characters.

In 1999–2000, a successful revival of the first of these played in both London and New York. According to one reviewer, "The Royal Shakespeare Company has struck gold where one wouldn't expect to find it. T. S. Eliot's *The Family Reunion* has a somewhat faded reputation. The shadow of Eng Lit hangs over it; in terms of theatrical history, it has come to look like an experiment on a road which wasn't leading anywhere. But in Adrian Noble's admirable production . . . it proves curiously compelling. . . . Fortunately, Noble's production brings out its strengths and as far as possible plays down its weaknesses."[19]

Perhaps there is life in Eliot's drama yet, but within a few years of his death in 1965, even Browne—his theatrical collaborator, friend, and greatest fan—was of two minds about Eliot's theatrical product: "I am sure that these plays will be found to have a permanent place in the repertory of English drama. Yet I feel that, by adopting [a] pattern of ironic social comedy, Eliot placed upon his genius a regrettable limitation. He tied himself to social, and still more to theatrical, conventions which were already outworn when the plays were written."[20] Eliot scholar Helen Gardner also noted the plays' many weaknesses, but shared Browne's possibly over-optimistic view that despite these flaws, "I cannot believe that *The Cocktail Party* and *The Confidential Clerk* will not find a place in the national repertory of the future."[21]

Less sympathetic still to the plays were some of the reviewers of *The Waste Land: A Facsimile*, upon its publication in 1971. One spoke of "Eliot's instinct for drama, so much more effective [in *The Waste Land*] than it usually is in his plays."[22] Another was much more biting: "The embarrassments of the plays are beyond comment."[23] An encyclopedia of modern world drama published the following year gave a fuller if equally negative assessment of Eliot's plays: "Eliot produced drama that is often obscure in plot and rarely sustains the wit of first-rate drawing-room comedy. The characterizations are too flat and the situations too vague to be impressive as spiritual examples. . . . Similarly, the language, when it does occasionally become unmistakably poetic, is embarrassingly out of place. . . ."[24]

Probably the most successful of the plays was *The Cocktail Party*, which was first produced in 1949. Its success may owe something to the fact that shortly before it opened, Eliot was honored with the 1948 Nobel Prize for Literature. Eliot worked on the play while serving as poet in-residence at the prestigious Institute for Advanced Study in Princeton, New Jersey, in fall 1948. The director of the Institute, J. Robert Oppenheimer, was a physicist who became famous for heading the scientific development of the atomic bomb during World War II. In 1922, the year *The Waste Land* was published, Oppenheimer had been a freshman and aspiring poet at Harvard. Oppenheimer later recalled, "I invited Eliot here in the hope that he would produce another masterpiece, and all he did was to work on *The Cocktail Party*, the worst thing he ever wrote."[25]

Shortly after the centennial celebration of Eliot's birth in 1988, another damning assessment of the plays appeared: "Read now, these later plays are unmistakably dead, embalmed, dated beyond endurance."[26] As the author of this piece noted, what remains of greatest interest to many in Eliot's plays today is the search for autobiographical references to the several women in his life. That this is so is proof that—unlike the case of *The Waste Land*—Eliot was unable in the plays to transform the particulars of his life into universal art. "As playwright, Eliot inexplicably . . . could not pull off his theory of demarcation between 'the man who suffers and the mind which creates,' so the plays are surprisingly confessional."[27] In *The Family Reunion*, for example, it is hard not to focus on the conviction of the protagonist, Harry, that he pushed his wife overboard to her death as they sailed the Atlantic, or on the discovery that Harry's father had long ago wanted to kill Harry's dominating mother so that he could marry her sister, Harry's Aunt Agatha. One need not stretch the imagination too far either to identify Emily Hale with Aunt Agatha, now an unmarried college teacher. Careful readers of *The Cocktail Party* may also note the inclusion in the text of the score for a song, with the caption, "The tune of *One-eyed Riley* (page 137), as scored from the author's dictation by Miss Mary Trevelyan."[28] Eliot also identified Mary Trevelyan with the play's Julia, a bossy busybody. In 1949, upon bumping into Trevelyan in a London pharmacy, Eliot is reported to have said, "Oh, it's you again, Julia."[29] Similarly, Eliot's relative success with the love poetry in his final play has been attributed to his entry into a happy second marriage while he was writing the play. In Eliot's *Collected Plays*, "To My Wife," later included as last of the occasional verses in *Collected Poems*, appears as a dedication to *The Elder Statesman*.[30]

CATS

Eliot did have a triumphant return to the stage in 1981, but from a totally unexpected quarter. In 1939 Faber & Faber published Eliot's *Old Possum's Book of Practical Cats*, a collection of humorous doggerel. Among the many people the light verses enchanted was composer Andrew Lloyd Webber, who began setting the poems to music in 1977. Valerie Eliot attended a 1980 summer festival where he performed some of these pieces. She brought with her some previously unpublished related pieces.

Two of these pieces in particular suggested a coherent plot for an evening's entertainment to Lloyd Webber and his eventual colleague Trevor Nunn. One was a poem "about a glamour cat," which Eliot described in a 1959 interview: "It turned out too sad. This would never do. I can't make my children weep over a cat who's gone wrong. She had a very questionable career, did this cat."[31]

But in "Grizabella the Glamour Cat," Lloyd Webber and Nunn saw the pivotal figure in a musical drama about redemption of the soul. Another piece Mrs. Eliot brought was a letter in which Eliot had mused about the cats' going "Up up up past the Russell Hotel, up up up to the Heaviside Layer." In the letter, Eliot proposed treating as a heavenly region this portion of the earth's upper atmosphere named for English physicist Oliver Heaviside (1850–1925). Nunn also drew from Eliot's early poem "Rhapsody on a Windy Night" to create the lyrics for "Memory," Grizabella's heartbreaking cry.[32]

What would T. S. Eliot have made of the success of this entertainment, in which the theme song's lyrics were not even his? In a 1962 letter he wrote, "I will not allow any of my poems to be set to music unless they seem to me to be lyrics in the proper sense of being suitable for singing."[33] Would the poems from *Old Possum's Book of Practical Cats* have met that criterion? Perhaps they would, and perhaps he would have found the musical not only delightful but also insightful. As one reviewer suggested, "'Cats' is lots of fun, but it also echoes something of a great poet's vision of loss and mortality. . . . Old Possum would have enjoyed the spectacle of his Grizabella escaping hell, rising to heaven amid a stageful of happy cats and a theaterful of happy people."[34]

TOM AND VIV

Whatever Eliot might have made of *Cats*, he would clearly not have been pleased with another play from the 1980s (or with its later movie version). In 1984, Eliot appeared onstage as one of the title characters in *Tom and Viv.* Playwright Michael Hastings based his script on a series of interviews he held with Vivien's younger brother over a period of several months in 1980, shortly before Maurice Haigh-Wood's death at the age of eighty-five.

Eliot would almost certainly have shared the opinion of his widow, who according to her former editorial assistant Karen Christensen, dismissed *Tom and Viv* as "that dreadful play."[35] What particularly irked Mrs. Eliot was Hastings's suggestion that Eliot conspired with the Haigh-Woods to have Vivien institutionalized in order to deprive her of her share of her father's estate. Valerie Eliot is not the only interested party to deny this allegation. Carole Seymour Jones, Vivien's sympathetic biographer, also asserts that Maurice, not Eliot, arranged for Vivien to be committed. She makes clear that whether or not Vivien was clinically insane in 1938, her behavior was so bizarre as to pose a threat to herself.

Despite or because of the controversy it aroused, Hastings's play earned some good reviews. One reviewer for *The New York Times,* for example, admired its "seven crisp scenes spanning the years 1915–1947," its "compassionate portrait of a tragic misalliance," and its guarantee "that Eliot is now remembered on the London stage as rather more than the author of a collection of jocular poems about cats."[36] In fall 2006 the play was revived in London, testifying to an enduring interest in Eliot's private life.

THE POET AS CRITIC

Examining Eliot's Essays

On September 14, 1964, at the American embassy in London, T. S. Eliot was honored with the Presidential Medal of Freedom, America's highest civilian award. The citation read, "Poet and critic, he has fused intelligence and imagination, tradition and innovation, bringing to the world a new sense of the possibilities in a revolutionary time."[1]

Over the course of his career, Eliot wrote many more lines of literary criticism than of poetry or drama, or even of poetry and drama combined. It is worth noting, too, that Eliot made his name as a critic well before he was known as a poet. The younger scholar F. W. Bateson (1901–1978) later recalled the impact of Eliot's first book of essays on Oxford undergraduates when it was published in 1920: "Until the publication of *The Waste Land* we were hardly aware of Eliot the poet, whereas we were very much aware of Eliot the critic. *The Sacred Wood* was almost our sacred book."[2]

In March 1919, more than a half year before *The Sacred Wood* appeared, Eliot wrote his mother, "There is a small and select public which regards me as the best

living critic, as well as the best living poet, in England. . . .
I really think that I have far more *influence* on English letters than any other American has ever had. . . . All this
sounds very conceited, but I am sure it is true. . . ."[3]

ELIOT'S CRITICISM AS A GUIDE TO HIS POEMS

Even though Eliot is no longer as revered a critic as he
once was, a knowledge of his criticism can help readers of
his poetry today. In the first essay in *The Sacred Wood*, "The
Perfect Critic," Eliot writes, "in matters of great importance the critic must not coerce, and he must not make
judgments of worse and better. He must simply elucidate:
the reader will form the correct judgment for himself."[4]
Readers today should keep this comment in mind as reassurance: The "correct judgment" of poems by Eliot or
anyone else is the one that they will reach after careful
reading.

In an essay on the French poet Baudelaire who had so
influenced Eliot's early poetry, Eliot wrote, "It is now
becoming understood that Baudelaire is one of the few
poets who wrote nothing, either prose or verse that is neg-
ligible. To understand Baudelaire you must read the whole
of Baudelaire. And nothing that he wrote is without
importance. He was a great poet; he was a great critic.
And he was also a man with a profound attitude toward
life, for the study of which we need every scrap of writing."[5] Similarly, those who wish to understand Eliot

would do well to sample all types of his writing, even if reading every scrap seems too daunting.

FAMOUS TERMS

In his 1956 essay "The Frontiers of Criticism," Eliot wrote, "The best of my *literary* criticism—apart from a few notorious phrases which have had a truly embarrassing success in the world—consists of essays on poets and poetic dramatists who had influenced me."[6] What were some of these "notorious phrases" that so embarrassed Eliot?

"OBJECTIVE CORRELATIVE"

Eliot, then an unknown foreign-born bank clerk in his early thirties, had the boldness not only to write about Shakespeare's *Hamlet* before he was an established poet himself but also to call it a "failure."[7] In his 1919 essay "Hamlet and His Problems" Eliot introduced the term "objective correlative" to explain Shakespeare's failure to convey "the inexpressibly horrible" emotion driving the play's protagonist.[8] According to Eliot, in his more successful plays, Shakespeare succeeded in making an "exact equivalence" between action and emotion, something he failed to do in *Hamlet*.[9] Eliot argued, "The only way of expressing emotion in the form of art is by finding an 'objective correlative'; in other words, a set of objects, a situation, a chain of events which shall be the formula of that *particular* emotion; such that when the external facts, which must terminate in sensory experience, are given, the emotion is immediately evoked."[10]

Eliot related Shakespeare's failure to find an objective correlative for Hamlet's emotion to what he considered that play's failure: "Hamlet (the man) is dominated by an emotion which is inexpressible, because it is in excess of the facts as they appear. . . . Hamlet's bafflement at the absence of objective equivalent to his feelings is a prolongation of the bafflement of his creator in the face of his artistic problem."[11] Eliot concluded, "We must simply admit that here Shakespeare tackled a problem which proved too much for him. Why he attempted it at all is an insoluble puzzle. . . ."[12]

It is interesting to note that a reviewer of Eliot's *The Family Reunion* used Eliot's own term and own argument to find fault with the play:

> He spoke in an essay once of Hamlet being dominated by an emotion which is inexpressible, because it is in excess of the facts as they appear. And the supposed identity of Hamlet with his author is genuine to this point; that Hamlet's bafflement at the absence of objective equivalent to his feelings is a prolongation of the bafflement of his creator in the face of his artistic problem. His own words describe the impression that "The Family Reunion" makes.[13]

Whether Eliot liked it or not, his term "objective correlative" took on a life of its own. In a 1965 edition of *The*

Reader's Encyclopedia, for example, the term has its own entry: "A phrase coined by T. S. Eliot in his essay *Hamlet* (1919). The term refers to the external equivalent of an inner emotional reality. Thus a scene, action, image, verse rhythm, or any other artistic device that expresses a subjective state may be regarded as its objective correlative."[14]

"DISSOCIATION OF SENSIBILITY"

That same encyclopedia also includes an entry for "dissociation of sensibility," another term whose success Eliot found embarrassing: "A phrase coined by T. S. Eliot in *The Metaphysical Poets* (1921). According to Eliot, the 17th-century poets could 'feel their thought as immediately as the odour of a rose,' but after them a 'dissociation of sensibility' set in and poets became either intellectual or emotional, but not both. Like the French symbolists, Eliot was trying to recapture that lost fusion of thought and feeling."[15]

In a memorable passage in his essay "The Metaphysical Poets," Eliot in effect describes a successful poet's unified sensibility, which permits the yoking together of seemingly unrelated experiences: "When a poet's mind is perfectly equipped for its work, it is constantly amalgamating disparate experience; the ordinary man's experience is chaotic, irregular, fragmentary. The latter falls in love, or reads Spinoza, and these two experiences have nothing to do with each other, or with the noise of the typewriter or the smell of cooking; in

the mind of the poet these experiences are always forming new wholes."

"IMPERSONALITY OF THE AUTHOR"

Two other terms associated with Eliot's criticism are
"impersonal poetry" and "tradition." *The Reader's
Encyclopedia* entry for Eliot's essay "Tradition and the
Individual Talent" refers to both concepts: "In this influential poetic manifesto the author asserts that a poet
cannot write significant poetry in the 20th century unless
he is steeped in the tradition and poetry of the past. The
past will teach him to avoid romantic, autobiographical
writing, and to concentrate on technique and impersonal,
detached poetry."[16]

In the essay, Eliot stresses that "The emotion of art is
impersonal. And the poet cannot reach this impersonality
without surrendering himself wholly to the work to be
done," that a true work of art requires "a continual extinc-
tion of [the author's] personality," that readers
must direct their attention not to "the poet" but to the
"poetry," and that "Poetry is not a turning loose of
emotion, but an escape from emotion; it is not the expres-
sion of personality, but an escape from personality."[17]

Eliot also wrote about the "impersonality of the poet"
in other essays. For example, in another essay from 1919,
on the English poet and playwright Ben Jonson
(1572–1637), Eliot wrote, "The creation of a work of

art . . . consists in the process of transfusion of the personality, or, in a deeper sense, the life of the author into the character."[18] In his 1927 essay "Shakespeare and the Stoicism of Seneca," he described Shakespeare's "struggle . . . to transmute his personal and private agonies into something rich and strange, something universal and impersonal."[19] In a 1940 essay on the Irish poet Yeats, Eliot talked about the "impersonality . . . of the poet who, out of intense and personal experience, is able to express a general truth; retaining all the particularity of his experience, to make of it a general symbol."[20]

"TRADITION"

Although Eliot was hardly the first critic to write about literary tradition, the concept played a particularly important role in his criticism. In "Tradition and the Individual Talent," Eliot criticized the "tendency to insist, when we praise a poet, upon those aspects of his work in which he least resembles any one else." He asserted that it is better to acknowledge that "not only the best, but the most individual parts of his work may be those in which the dead poets, his ancestors, assert their immortality most vigorously." The essay also argued that a poet who seeks to become part of tradition can do so only through "great labour," involving "the historical sense, which . . . compels a man to write not merely with his own generation in his bones, but with a feeling that the whole of the literature of Europe from Homer and within it the whole of the literature of his own country has a simultaneous existence and composes a simultaneous order."[21]

In the same essay Eliot asserted not only that "the poet must develop or procure the consciousness of the past" but also "that he should continue to develop this consciousness throughout his career."[22] Eliot certainly seemed steeped enough in the past to readers of *The Waste Land* less familiar than he was with the literary tradition. Nonetheless, shortly after completing the poem, he expressed his belief that his consciousness of the past was insufficient. At the end of December 1922 he wrote his brother, "what I particularly long for is time to fill in the innumerable gaps in my education in past literature and history."[23] He longed to practice what he preached.

THE WASTE LAND THROUGH THE LENS OF ELIOT'S CRITICISM

Eliot's critical essays did more than guide readers through the work of the poets on whom they focused. They also helped make readers appreciate his own revolutionary poetry. In "Tradition and the Individual Talent," Eliot argued that ". . . what happens when a new work of art is created is something that happens simultaneously to all the works of art which preceded it. . . the past should be altered by the present as much as the present is directed by the past."[24] In other words, Eliot's work transformed the way previous works were read. Once *The Waste Land* incorporated quotations from past literature, those works could never be looked at in the same way as they had before his poem was published.

In an essay written in 1920, before *The Waste Land* was finished, Eliot shed light on what would become one of the defining characteristics of that poem: its inclusion of direct quotations from (and allusions to) past works of literature. He wrote:

> One of the surest of tests is the way in which a poet borrows. Immature poets imitate; mature poets steal; bad poets deface what they take, and good poets make it into something better, or at least something different. The good poet welds his theft into a whole of feeling which is unique, utterly different from that from which it was torn; the bad poet throws it into something which has no cohesion. A good poet will usually borrow from authors remote in time, or alien in language, or diverse in interest.[25]

By his own definition, in *The Waste Land* he proved himself a mature poet and a good one.

In a 1929 essay on Dante, Eliot wrote:

> The experience of a poem is the experience both of a moment and of a lifetime. . . . There is a first, or an early moment which is unique, of shock and surprise, even of terror. . . . a moment which can never be forgotten, but which is never repeated integrally; and yet which would become destitute of significance if it did not survive in a larger whole of experience. . . . The majority of poems one outgrows

and outlives, as one outgrows and outlives the majority of human passions.[26]

Individual readers of Eliot's *The Waste Land* must discover for themselves whether it is a poem that remains meaningful for them throughout their lives.

Eliot later claimed that despite what "various critics" might have said, far from setting out to write a "criticism of the contemporary world," *The Waste Land* to him "was only the relief of a personal and wholly insignificant grouse against life; . . . just a piece of rhythmical grumbling."[27] Nonetheless, a few years after *The Waste Land* was written, Eliot effectively described his own achievement in an essay about Shakespeare:

> The great poet, in writing himself, writes his time. Thus Dante, hardly knowing it, became the voice of the thirteenth century; Shakespeare, hardly knowing it, became the representative of the end of the sixteenth century, of a turning point in history.[28]

Whatever standing Eliot ultimately achieves in the ranks of English-language poets, it seems likely that *The Waste Land* will remain representative of the turning point in history that World War I marked.

POET FOR OUR CENTURY?

The Final Years and Lasting Legacy of T. S. Eliot

T S. Eliot's first marriage to Vivien had not brought him happiness. During his separation from Vivien he had become close to two other women, the American Emily Hale and the English Mary Trevelyan. Each woman hoped to become the second Mrs. Eliot, should the opportunity arise. Vivien's death on January 23, 1947, however, did not result in the outcome either woman desired.

Almost a decade later, however, even Eliot's closest friends were taken by surprise when on January 10, 1957, he married Valerie Fletcher. Fletcher, born in 1926, had idolized Eliot since hearing a recording of one of his poems as a teenager. Before turning twenty-five she had landed the position of private secretary to her hero. Now, at the age of thirty, she became the wife of the sixty-eight-year-old man who, in turn, worshipped her.

THE BEST YEARS

For the first time in his life Eliot seemed truly happy. His editor Robert Giroux later recalled, "'Radiant' may seem an odd word to apply to T. S. Eliot, yet it is an accurate description of the last eight or so years of his life, and this was due of course to his marriage in 1957 to Valerie Fletcher. More than once in those years I heard him utter the words, 'I'm the luckiest man in the world.'"[1]

Eliot had never enjoyed robust health, and as he grew older the periods of illness became more frequent. Occasionally his illnesses made the news. In June 1956, for example, he fell ill while sailing back to England following his annual trip to the United States. Upon his arrival on the *Queen Mary*, the United Press issued a report under the headline, "Exhausted T. S. Eliot Rushed to Hospital."[2] Despite his periodic illnesses, however, Eliot maintained a rather full schedule through 1963. As his theatrical producer E. Martin Browne noted, "he did not undertake any further major writing" following his last play, *The Elder Statesman*, which appeared in 1958.[3] Nonetheless, every autumn he and Valerie traveled to the United States, where Eliot lectured and gave poetry readings. Before returning to London they would spend some of the winter in the Bahamas or the Caribbean. In early summer 1963, months after a five-week hospitalization, Eliot wrote the younger poet Donald Hall that while still not fully recovered, he was able to work three afternoons a week in his office. That fall, Faber & Faber marked his seventy-fifth birthday by publishing his *Collected Poems 1909–1962*.

One of Valerie Eliot's editorial assistants later described Mrs. Eliot's efforts to guard her husband "from

London smog and from reporters who booked seats behind them on a holiday flight to the Bahamas."[4] In fact, the Eliots' last extensive trip was their sojourn in the Bahamas in winter 1963–1964. Eliot was too ill to travel to Washington, D.C., to receive the Presidential Medal of Freedom from his native land in 1964. The award was bestowed upon him instead at the American Embassy in London that September.

MOURNING T. S. ELIOT

Though it was clear to all that Eliot was in declining health, his death still came as a blow to his friends. Browne recalled, "It was sad, as we met again each summer, to see him decline in strength: but we had the joy of seeing also that his happiness deepened with every year. Our last meeting was on 2 September 1964. . . . He was very frail; and yet it was a numbing shock to hear over the radio, at midnight on 4 January 1965, that he had died."[5]

A variety of tributes to Eliot were held throughout 1965. On the month anniversary of his death, a memorial service at Westminster Abbey—the great national church near the Houses of Parliament in London—was attended by dignitaries from many countries. A statement from United States President Lyndon Johnson was read aloud: "The President wishes to pay tribute to a poet and playwright who had a profound impact on his times and who achieved distinction on both sides of the Atlantic."[6] The choir sang the anthem "The Dove Descending," a musical arrangement by Russian-born composer Igor Stravinsky (1882–1971) of Part IV of Eliot's *Little Gidding*. Eliot and Stravinsky, one of the most influential composers of the 1900s, had been acquainted since 1956, when the composer invited the poet to tea at a London hotel. On the second anniversary of Eliot's death, a memorial stone was placed in the floor of Westminster Abbey in his memory.

Eliot's body was cremated. In April 1965, his ashes were taken to St. Michael's Church, East Coker, the ancestral village that had inspired the second of Eliot's *Four Quartets*. In September 1965, English publisher Sir Rupert Hart-Davis (1907–1999) memorialized Eliot at East Coker. Hart-Davis recalled that for years Eliot was "almost as much sought after as a Beatle. He had to keep his address secret, remove his telephone number from the book, and set up an elaborate system of defenses against the army of admirers, journalists, professors and students" who tried to track him down.[7]

Churches were not the only venues for tributes to Eliot. The University of Kent, a new academic institution in Canterbury, opened its first college in 1965. The university named it after Eliot, whose 1935 *Murder in the Cathedral* had dramatized a significant moment in Canterbury's illustrious history. On June 13, 1965, there was a gathering in his honor at the Globe Theatre in London. Among the actors who read works by Eliot was American comedian Groucho Marx (1890–1977), with whom Eliot struck up an unlikely friendship and correspondence in 1961. The performance of *Sweeney Agonistes* on that occasion led to a London revival of Eliot's first theatrical work the following winter.

In his condolence note to Valerie Eliot, American poet Robert Lowell voiced a sentiment that many other Eliot friends and colleagues also expressed: "I'm sure everyone tells you that you gave Tom his greatest happiness. We all think this. Somehow I think, the long spiritual pilgrimage, that gruelling, heroic and yet inwardly at peace exploration and purgation—all that shines through *Ash Wednesday* and the *Quartets* was inevitably going to end in the surprise reward of a joyfull [*sic*] marriage."[8]

POSTHUMOUS PUBLICATIONS

It was to be expected that in the decades following Eliot's death many books about him and his work would be published. Less expected, however, was the publication in 1971 of a facsimile edition of the recently discovered manuscripts of *The Waste Land*, which had been marked up by Ezra Pound, Vivien Eliot, and Eliot himself. As Ezra Pound noted in his preface to the volume, "The more we know of Eliot, the better. I am thankful that the lost leaves have been unearthed." Pound also paid homage to Eliot's widow, who established herself with this volume as a meticulous editor: "Valerie Eliot has done a scholarly job which would have delighted her husband. For this, and for her patience with my attempts to elucidate my own marginal notes, and for the kindness which distinguishes her, I express my thanks.[9]

Mrs. Eliot continued to apply her scholarly skills to her husband's correspondence. In 1988, the year that marked the centennial of T. S. Eliot's birth, she issued the first of what she promised would be several volumes of his correspondence. In her introduction she described the genesis of the project. "At the time of our marriage in 1957 I was dismayed to learn that my husband had forbidden the future publication of his correspondence, because I appreciated its importance and fascination. As he often read aloud to me in the evenings . . . I took every opportunity to introduce a poet's letters, until, eventually, he burst out laughing, and said he would relent on condition that I did the selecting and editing."[10]

The epigraph Mrs. Eliot selected for her collection of letters also suggests that her husband understood and perhaps shared the mixed feelings about the privacy of personal letters that he attributed to other writers. Opposite the copyright page she included a remark her brother-in-law, Henry Eliot, recorded from an unpreserved lecture, "English Poets as Letter Writers," which Eliot presented at Yale University in November 1933: "The desire to write a letter, to put down what you don't want anybody else to see but the person you are writing to, but which you do not want to be destroyed, but perhaps hope may be preserved for complete strangers to read, is ineradicable. We want to confess ourselves in writing to a few friends, and we do not always want to feel that no one but those friends will ever read what we have written."[11]

Although Valerie Eliot expressed her intention to publish a second volume of Eliot's letters in 1989, no subsequent volumes have appeared. In 1996, however, those eager for more unpublished work by Eliot found some consolation when *The Inventions of the March Hare*, the contents of the recently discovered notebook of his early poems, was published.

Because Valerie Eliot holds the rights to all of her husband's work, she has been able to control certain aspects of Eliot scholarship. She has not been able, however, to keep scholars and popularizers from offering assessments of Eliot and his work that doubtless deviate from her own. Despite her disparagement of Michael Hastings's 1980s play, a film version *Tom & Viv* was released in 1994. In reviewing the film for *The New York Times*, Caryn James called Eliot "an enduring poet and a horrid individual."[12] Nor was Valerie Eliot able to keep old accusations of anti-Semitism from resurfacing. *T. S. Eliot, Anti-Semitism, and Literary Form*, by English lawyer Anthony Julius, stimulated much scholarly debate from the late 1990s into the twenty-first century about Eliot's attitude toward Jews.

Eliot's centennial year, 1988, must have been a painful one for Mrs. Eliot in some respects, as it led some highly respected literary critics to make damaging remarks about Eliot. Robert Alter (b. 1935), for example, acknowledged that Eliot was "the definitively modern poet in English." By pointing out Eliot's "narrow range" and mere "trickle of poems," however, Alter insisted that Eliot was far from the "greatest" or "most original" poet of his period. Alter clearly felt empathy for Eliot, who "deserves a measure of compassion, for he was able to produce a few of the trail-blazing English poems of the century only at a terrible personal cost." This assessment, however, is far from a resounding affirmation of Eliot's greatness.[13] Similarly, Cynthia Ozick (b. 1928) marked Eliot's centennial by writing in a long and hostile article in *The New Yorker*, "we no longer live in the literary shadow of T. S. Eliot."[14]

TIME WILL TELL

Eliot scholar Helen Gardner made a comment about Eliot's comedies that bears upon the question of Eliot's literary legacy in general: "I cannot take very seriously a criticism that assumes that what is temporarily unfashionable is permanently out of date."[15]

As this book goes to press, the jury is still out on the ultimate place Eliot's work will find in the history of English literature. On New Year's Day 2006, an article in *The Boston Globe* suggested that "the circumspect closing passage of *The New York Times* obituary that ran forty years ago last January almost might have been written yesterday: 'Although Eliot's influence began to wane in the last decade of his life, we are still too close to the light he shed to take his measure accurately.'"[16]

When Eliot died, American poet and critic John Crowe Ransom (1888–1974) wrote, "We must re-read him, and think a long time about his achievement, and about how the parts cumulated into a whole; thinking as precisely as we could possibly think about something intangible, in order to say what he had meant to English letters."[17] A new generation of readers has now become what Ransom called "the executors who must appraise the estate" that Eliot left behind.

To assess Eliot's legacy, his twenty-first century readers will have to rely on their own responses. Perhaps they will conclude that the poet who combated his own internal terrors during an age that experienced two world wars, savage genocide, and the introduction of nuclear weaponry, is still a meaningful poet for an age filled with challenges of its own.

CHRONOLOGY

1888—*September 26:* Thomas Stearns Eliot is born in St. Louis, Missouri.

1905–1906—Does a postgraduate year at Milton Academy, a prestigious New England boarding school.

1906–1909—Earns A.B. at Harvard College in three years.

1909–1910—Studies for a master's degree in English literature at Harvard.

1910–1911—Spends nine months in Paris; in July, before returning to the United States, completes the final version of "The Love Song of J. Alfred Prufrock."

1911–1914—Graduate student in philosophy at Harvard University.

1914—Departs for Europe on traveling fellowship.

1915—*June:* "The Love Song of J. Alfred Prufrock" is published in *Poetry*; marries Vivienne Haigh-Wood.

September 1915–1916—Schoolmaster at High Wycombe and in Highgate.

June 1916—Harvard accepts his doctoral thesis in philosophy; Eliot turns down the offer of an academic career there.

1916–1919—Lecturer at five college-level extension courses.

1917–1925—Works at Lloyds Bank in the city of London.

1917—*Prufrock and Other Observations* is published.

1922—Becomes famous after *The Waste Land* is published.

1922–1939—Edits a literary journal, *The Criterion*.

1923–1956—Friendship with Emily Hale.

1925—Becomes director of new publishing firm, Faber & Gwyer (the name is changed in 1929 to Faber & Faber).

1927—Baptized into the Church of England and exchanges American for British nationality.

1932–1933—Takes up Charles Eliot Norton Professorship at Harvard for academic year, effectively separating from Vivienne.

1938—Vivienne Eliot is committed to an asylum, where she spends the rest of her life.

1938–1956—Friendship with Mary Trevelyan.

1943—*Four Quartets* published for the first time as a complete sequence in the United States.

1947—Vivienne, age fifty-eight, dies suddenly of heart failure; Eliot is granted an honorary doctorate from Harvard in mid-June.

1948—Visiting Fellow at the Institute for Advanced Study in Princeton, New Jersey; is awarded in January the Order of Merit, the highest honor the British monarch could bestow on him, and in December the Nobel Prize for Literature.

1957—*January 10:* Marries Valerie Fletcher.

1964—Awarded United States Presidential Medal of Freedom.

1965—*January 4:* Dies in London.

1967—*January 4:* Memorial stone in Eliot's memory placed in floor of Westminster Abbey.

1971—*The Waste Land: A Facsimile and Transcript of the Original Drafts Including the Annotations of Ezra Pound* is published.

1981–1982—*Cats*, Andrew Lloyd Webber's hit musical based on *Old Possum's Book of Practical Cats*, opens in London and New York.

1986—The United States Postal Service issues a 22-cent stamp in honor of T. S. Eliot.

1988—Centennial celebrations in New York and London; *The Letters of T. S. Eliot, Volume One, 1898–1922*, is published.

1996—*Inventions of the March Hare*, a collection of poems Eliot wrote between 1909 and 1917, is published for the first time.

1998—Selected by *Time* magazine as one of the hundred most important people of the twentieth century.

CHAPTER NOTES

CHAPTER 1. POET OF HIS CENTURY?

1. Robert Alter, "What Was T. S. Eliot?" *Commentary,* March 1989, p. 31.

2. *The Concise Oxford Dictionary of Literary Terms* (New York: Oxford University Press, 1991), s.v., "modernism."

3. Helen Vendler, review of *The Waste Land: A Facsimile and Transcript of the Original Drafts* (New York: Harcourt Brace Jovanovich, 1971), *The New York Times Book Review*, November 7, 1971, p. 1.

4. Hugh Kenner, *The Invisible Poet: T. S. Eliot* (New York: McDowell, Obolensky, 1959), p. 106.

5. Caroline Behr, *T. S. Eliot: A Chronology of His Life and Works* (New York: St. Martin's Press, 1983), p. 68.

6. Vendler, p. 45.

7. Roger Kimball, "A Craving for Reality: T. S. Eliot Today," *The New Criterion*, October 1999, <http://www.newcriterion.com/archive/18/oct99/eliot.htm> (June 4, 2007).

8. T. S. Eliot, *The Use of Poetry and the Use of Criticism* (London: Faber & Faber Limited, 1933), p. 154.

9. Helen Vendler, "T. S. Eliot," Artists & Entertainers of the 20th Century, *Time*, June 8, 1998, p. 111.

10. Ibid., p. 112.

11. A. David Moody, ed., *The Cambridge Companion to T. S. Eliot* (Cambridge, U.K.: Cambridge University Press, 1994), p. xiii.

12. T. S. Eliot, *Inventions of the March Hare: Poems 1909–1917*, ed. Christopher Ricks (New York: Harcourt Brace & Company, 1996), p. xix.

13. Behr, p. 66.

14. T. S. Eliot, "Dante," in *Selected Essays, 1917–1932* (New York: Harcourt, Brace & World, Inc., 1960), p. 200.

15. E. Martin Browne, *The Making of T. S. Eliot's Plays* (Cambridge, U.K.: Cambridge University Press, 1969), p. 2.

16. T. S. Eliot, *Inventions of the March Hare: Poems 1909–1917*, p. xxvi.

17. T. S. Eliot, *To Criticize the Critic* (New York: Farrar, Straus & Giroux, 1965), pp. 22–23.

18. Edmund Wilson, "The Poetry of Drouth," *The Dial*, December 1922, vol. LXXIII, pp. 611–616. Quoted in *T. S. Eliot: The Critical Heritage*, ed. Michael Grant, vol. 1 (London: Routledge & Kegan Paul, 1982), pp. 143–144.

19. Virginia Woolf, quoted in James E. Miller, Jr., *T. S. Eliot: The Making of an American Poet*, 1888–1922 (University Park, Pa.: The Pennsylvania State University Press, 2005), p. 396.

20. T. S. Eliot, "The Social Function of Poetry," in *On Poetry and Poets* (New York: Farrar, Straus & Giroux, 1957), p. 12.

21. "Defiant Moussaoui Gets Life Term," *The New York Times*, <http://www.nytimes.com/reuters/news/news-security-moussaoui.html?_r=1&oref=slogin&pagewanted=print> (May 4, 2006).

22. Manohla Dargis and A. O. Scott, "Cannes Notebook: Dystopia, Widows, Da Vinci and Sex at Cannes Festival," *The New York Times*, May 22, 2006, <http://select.nytimes.com/search/restricted/article?res=F30E11FF3B5A0C718EDDAC0894DE404482> (June 4, 2007).

23. T. S. Eliot, *Collected Poems 1909–1962* (New York: Harcourt Brace Jovanovich, 1963), p. 53.

24. Rick Lyman, "School's Waning Days," *The New York Times*, June 22, 2006, <http://www.nytimes.com/2006/06/22/nyregion/22june.html?_r=1&oref=slogin&pagewanted=print> (June 23, 2006).

25. T. S. Eliot, *Collected Poems 1909–1962*, p. 5.

26. Hugh Kenner, "Old Possum's Postbag," *The New York Times Book Review*, October 16, 1988, p. 41.

CHAPTER 2. THE MARCH HARE

1. T. S. Eliot, "Tradition and the Individual Talent," in *Selected Essays, 1917–1932* (New York: Harcourt, Brace & World, Inc., 1960), p. 7.

2. Peter Ackroyd, *T. S. Eliot: A Life* (New York: Simon and Schuster, 1984), p. 335.

3. Sir Herbert Read, "T. S. E.—A Memoir," in *T. S. Eliot: The Man and His Work*, ed. Allen Tate (New York: Delacorte Press, 1966), p. 15.

4. Valerie Eliot, ed., *The Letters of T. S. Eliot*, Volume I, 1898–1922 (New York: Harcourt Brace Jovanovich, Publishers, 1988), p. xxxi.

5. Cleo McNelly Kearns, "Religion, Literature, and Society in the Work of T. S. Eliot," *The Cambridge Companion to T. S. Eliot*, ed. A. David Moody (Cambridge, U.K.: Cambridge University Press, 1994), p. 88.

6. James E. Miller, Jr., *T. S. Eliot: The Making of an American Poet, 1888–1922* (University Park, Pa.: The Pennsylvania State University Press, 2005), p. 11.

7. Letter of October 15, 1930, to Marquis Childs of the *St. Louis Post-Dispatch*. Quoted in Miller, p. 27.

8. T. S. Eliot, *The Use of Poetry and the Use of Criticism: Studies in the Relation of Criticism to Poetry in England* (London: Faber &Faber Limited, 1933), p. 33.

9. Quoted in Miller, p. 6.

10. Donald Hall, "T. S. Eliot," *Writers at Work: The* Paris

Review *Interviews*, Second Series, Introduced by Van Wyck Brooks (New York: The Viking Press, 1963), pp. 92–93.

11. Cleanth Brooks, "T. S. Eliot: Thinker and Artist," in *T. S. Eliot: The Man and His Work*, ed. Allen Tate (New York: Delacorte Press, 1966), p. 317.

12. T. S. Eliot, *To Criticize the Critic* (London: Faber & Faber, 1965), p. 126. Quoted in Ronald Schuchard, *Eliot's Dark Angel: Intersections of Life and Art* (New York: Oxford University Press, 1999), p. 70.

13. T. S. Eliot, "A Commentary," *The Criterion*, April 1934, Vol. XIII, p. 451.

14. Lyndall Gordon, *T. S. Eliot: An Imperfect Life* (New York: W. W. Norton & Company, 1999), p. 46.

15. Quoted in Miller, p. 147.

16. Hall, pp. 98–99.

17. Valerie Eliot, p. 13.

18. T. S. Eliot, "The Love Song of J. Alfred Prufrock," *Collected Poems 1909–1962* (New York: Harcourt Brace Jovanovich, 1963), pp. 3, 4.

19. T. S. Eliot, "Afternoon," *Inventions of the March Hare*, ed. Christopher Ricks (New York: Harcourt Brace & Company, 1996), p. 53.

20. "Annotations for *The Love Song of J. Alfred Prufrock*," from B. C. Southam, *A Guide to the Selected Poems of T. S. Eliot* (New York: Harcourt, Brace & World, 1968), <http://www.geocities.com/Athens/Acropolis/5616/annotati.html> (June 4, 2007).

21. Dana Gioia, "Eliot Uncovered," *The Washington Times*, March 16, 1997, <http://www.danagioia.net/essays/eeliot.htm> (June 4, 2007).

CHAPTER 3. MOMENTOUS CHANGES

1. Recollections of Aiken and Pound quoted in James E. Miller, Jr., *T. S. Eliot: The Making of an American Poet*,

1888–1922 (University Park, Pa.: The Pennsylvania State University Press, 2005), p. 198.

2. Donald Hall, "T. S. Eliot," *Writers at Work: The* Paris Review *Interviews*, Second Series, Introduced by Van Wyck Brooks (New York: The Viking Press, 1963), p. 95.

3. Valerie Eliot, ed., *The Letters of T. S. Eliot*, Volume I, 1898–1922 (New York: Harcourt Brace Jovanovich, Publishers, 1988), p. xvii.

4. James E. Miller, Jr., *T. S. Eliot: The Making of an American Poet, 1888–1922* (University Park, Pa.: The Pennsylvania State University Press, 2005), p. 119.

5. Valerie Eliot, p. 65.

6. Ibid., p. 74.

7. Ibid., p. 88.

8. Ibid., p. 97.

9. Helen Vendler, review of *The Waste Land: A Facsimile and Transcript of the Original Drafts* (New York: Harcourt Brace Jovanovich, 1971), *The New York Times Book Review*, November 7, 1971, p. 1.

10. Craig R. Whitney, "2 More T. S. Eliot Poems Found Amid Hundreds of His Letters," *The New York Times*, November 2, 1991, <http://select.nytimes.com/search/restricted/article?res=F20610FA355A0C718CDDA80994D94> (June 4, 2007).

11. Valerie Eliot, p. xvii.

12. *The Autobiography of Bertrand Russell, 1914–1944* (Boston: Little, Brown and Company, 1968), p. 63.

13. Ibid., pp. 65–66.

14. Carole Seymour-Jones, *Painted Shadow: The Life of Vivienne Eliot, First Wife of T. S. Eliot, and the Long-suppressed Truth About Her Influence on His Genius* (New York: Doubleday, 2001), p. 110.

15. Ezra Pound to Henry Ware Eliot, postmarked June

28, 1915, Valerie Eliot, ed., *The Letters of T. S. Eliot*, Volume I, 1898–1922, p. 104.

16. Caroline Behr, *T. S. Eliot: A Chronology of His Life and Works* (New York: St. Martin's Press, 1983), p. 11.

17. Letter to Henry Eliot, November 5, 1916, Valerie Eliot, p. 157.

18. Valerie Eliot, p. 161.

19. Ronald Bush, *T. S. Eliot: A Study in Character and Style* (New York: Oxford University Press, 1983), p. 19.

20. Valerie Eliot, p. 171.

21. Hall, "T. S. Eliot," p. 106.

22. Valerie Eliot, p. 104.

23. Letter to Richard Aldington, November 6, 1921, Valerie Eliot, p. 486.

24. Julian Symons, *Makers of the New: The Revolution in Literature, 1912-1939* (New York: Random House, 1987), p. 83.

25. T. S. Eliot, *The Waste Land: A Facsimile and Transcript of the Original Drafts*, ed. Valerie Eliot (New York: Harcourt Brace Jovanovich, Inc., 1971), p. xii.

26. Valerie Eliot, p. 266.

27. Ibid., p. 151.

28. Ibid., p. 173.

29. Hall, "T. S. Eliot," p. 98.

30. T. S. Eliot, "Gerontion," *Collected Poems 1909–1962* (New York: Harcourt Brace Jovanovich, Publishers, 1963), p. 29.

31. Ibid., p. 30.

32. Valerie Eliot, p. xvii.

33. Lyndall Gordon, "Eliot and Women," in *T. S. Eliot: The Modernist in History,* ed. Ronald Bush (Cambridge, U.K.: Cambridge University Press, 1991), p. 12.

Chapter 4. The Breakout Poem

1. Valerie Eliot, ed., *The Letters of T. S. Eliot*, Volume I, 1898–1922 (New York: Harcourt Brace Jovanovich, Publishers, 1988), p. 344.

2. Ibid., p. 451.

3. Ibid., p. 441.

4. Ibid., p. 467.

5. Lawrence Rainey, ed., *The Annotated Waste Land with Eliot's Contemporary Prose* (New Haven: Yale University Press, 2005), p. 20.

6. Richard Ellmann, "The First Waste Land—I," *The New York Review of Books*, Vol. 17, No. 8, November 18, 1971, <http://www.nybooks.com/articles/10378> (March 5, 2006).

7. Valerie Eliot, p. 493.

8. Ibid., pp. 497–498.

9. Ibid., p. 498.

10. Ibid., p. 572.

11. T. S. Eliot, *Collected Poems 1909–1962* (New York: Harcourt Brace Jovanovich, Publishers, 1963), p. 53.

12. Ibid., p. 61.

13. Roger Kimball, "A Craving for Reality: T. S. Eliot Today," *The New Criterion*, October 1999, <http://www.newcriterion.com/archive/18/oct99/eliot.htm> (June 4, 2007).

14. T. S. Eliot, *Collected Poems 1909–1962*, p. 61.

15. The *Random House Dictionary of the English Language, Second Edition, Unabridged* (New York: Random House, 1987), s.v., "demotic," "vernacular."

16. Kimball.

17. Ellmann.

18. Donald Hall, "T. S. Eliot," *Writers at Work: The Paris Review Interviews*, Second Series, Introduced by Van Wyck Brook (New York: The Viking Press, 1963), p. 96.

19. "Seven Books of Special Significance Published in 1971," *The New York Times Book Review*, December 5, 1971, p. 2.

20. Valerie Eliot, p. 497.

21. Julian Symons, *Makers of the New: The Revolution in Literature, 1912–1939* (New York: Random House, 1987), p. 154.

22. T. S. Eliot, *Collected Poems 1909–1962*, p. 59.

23. T. S. Eliot, "Notes on 'The Waste Land,' *Collected Poems 1909–1962*, p. 70.

24. Hugh Kenner, *The Invisible Poet: T. S. Eliot* (New York: McDowell, Obolensky, 1959), pp. 151–152.

25. T. S. Eliot, "The Frontiers of Criticism," in *On Poetry and Poets* (New York: The Noonday Press, 1966), pp. 121–122.

26. Ronald Bush, *T. S. Eliot: A Study in Character and Style* (New York: Oxford University Press, 1983), p. 63.

27. T. S. Eliot, *Collected Poems 1909–1962*, p. 54.

28. Ibid., p. 57.

29. Lyndall Gordon, *T. S. Eliot: An Imperfect Life* (New York: W. W. Norton & Company, 1999), p. 116. Cf. T. S. Eliot, *Collected Poems 1909–1962*, p. 57.

30. Lyndall Gordon, "Eliot and Women," in *T. S. Eliot: The Modernist in History*, ed. Ronald Bush (Cambridge, U.K.: Cambridge University Press, 1991), p. 10.

31. T. S. Eliot, *Collected Poems 1909–1962*, p. 57.

32. Gordon, p. 169.

33. Jewel Spears Brooker and Joseph Bentley, *Reading The Waste Land: Modernism and the Limits of Interpretation* (Amherst: The University of Massachusetts Press, 1990), p. 171.

34. T. S. Eliot, *Collected Poems 1909–1962*, pp. 61, 62.

35. Ibid., pp. 56, 61.

36. Ibid., p. 63.

37. Brooker and Bentley, p. 161.

38. T. S. Eliot, *Collected Poems 1909–1962*, pp. 54, 57.

39. Ibid., p. 60.

40. Helen Gardner, *The Art of T. S. Eliot* (London: The Cresset Press, 1949), p. 95.

41. Ibid., p. 96.

42. T. S. Eliot, *Collected Poems 1909–1962*, p. 68.

43. Ibid., p. 67.

44. Letter to Bertrand Russell, October 15, 1923, in *The Autobiography of Bertrand Russell, 1914–1944* (Boston: Little, Brown and Company, 1968), p. 265.

45. James E. Miller Jr., *T. S. Eliot: The Making of an American Poet, 1888–1922* (University Park, Pa.: The Pennsylvania State University Press, 2005), p. 418.

46. T. S. Eliot, *Collected Poems 1909–1962*, p. 67.

47. Ibid., pp. 69, 76.

48. Kenner, p. 182.

49. Conrad Aiken, "An Anatomy of Melancholy," in *T. S. Eliot: The Man and His Work*, ed. Allen Tate (New York: Delacorte Press, 1966), p. 202.

50. Hall, p. 97.

51. T. S. Eliot, "Thoughts After Lambeth," in *Selected Essays*, New Edition (New York: Harcourt, Brace & World, Inc., 1960), p. 324.

52. T. S. Eliot, "Shakespeare and the Stoicism of Seneca," in *Selected Essays*, New Edition, p. 117.

53. Hall, p. 98.

54. Miller, pp. 410–411.

55. Bonamy Dobré, "T. S. Eliot: A Personal Reminiscence," in *T. S. Eliot: The Man and His Work*, ed. Allen Tate (New York: Delacorte Press, 1966), p. 76.

56. Miller, p. 406.

57. Bush, p. 103.

58. Valerie Eliot, p. 596.

CHAPTER 5. NEW IDENTITIES

1. Valerie Eliot, ed., *The Letters of T. S. Eliot*, Volume I, 1898–1922 (New York: Harcourt Brace Jovanovich, Publishers, 1988), p. 544.

2. Ibid., pp. 597–598.

3. Ronald Bush, *T. S. Eliot: A Study in Character and Style* (New York: Oxford University Press, 1983), p. 82.

4. Ibid., pp. 104–105.

5. Stephen Spender, "Remembering Eliot," in *T. S. Eliot: The Man and His Work*, ed. Allen Tate (New York: Delacorte Press, 1966), p. 56.

6. John Lehmann, "T. S. Eliot Talks About Himself and the Drive to Create," *The New York Times Book Review*, November 29, 1953, p. 5.

7. Donald Hall, "T. S. Eliot," *Writers at Work: The* Paris Review *Interviews*, Second Series, Introduced by Van Wyck Brook (New York: The Viking Press, 1963), p. 100.

8. T. S. Eliot, "The Hollow Men," *Collected Poems 1909–1962* (New York: Harcourt Brace Jovanovich, Publishers, 1963), p. 77.

9. T. S. Eliot, "The Waste Land," *Collected Poems 1909–1962*, p. 69.

10. T. S. Eliot, "The Hollow Men," *Collected Poems 1909–1962*, pp. 81–82.

11. Helen Gardner, *The Art of T. S. Eliot* (London: The Cresset Press, 1949), p. 105.

12. Ibid., p. 122.

13. T. S. Eliot, "Ash-Wednesday," *Collected Poems 1909–1962*, p. 95.

14. Ibid., p. 86.

15. T. S. Eliot, "Introduction," Djuna Barnes, *Nightwood* (New York: Harcourt, Brace, 1937), p. xii.

16. Sir Herbert Read, "T. S. E.–A Memoir," in *T. S. Eliot:*

The Man and His Work, ed. Allen Tate (New York: Delacorte Press, 1966), p. 15.

17. Craig R. Whitney, "2 More T. S. Eliot Poems Found Amid Hundreds of His Letters," *The New York Times*, November 2, 1991, <http://select.nytimes.com/search/restricted/article?res=F20610FA355A0C718CDDA80994D 94> (June 4, 2007).

18. James E. Miller, Jr., *T. S. Eliot: The Making of an American Poet, 1888–1922* (University Park, Pa.: The Pennsylvania State University Press, 2005), p. 424.

19. Caroline Behr, *T. S. Eliot: A Chronology of his Life and Works* (New York: St. Martin's Press, 1983), p. 35.

20. T. S. Eliot, "The Cultivation of Christmas Trees," *Collected Poems 1909–1962*, pp. 107–108.

21. J. C. C. Mays, "Early poems: From 'Prufrock' to 'Gerontion,'" ed. A. David Moody, *The Cambridge Companion to T. S. Eliot*, (Cambridge, U.K.: Cambridge University Press, 1994), p. 119.

22. Carole Seymour-Jones, *Painted Shadow The Life of Vivienne Eliot, First Wife of T. S. Eliot, and the Long-Suppressed Truth About Her Influence on His Genius* (New York: Doubleday, 2001), p. 448.

23. Bush, p. 104.

24. Ibid., p. 102.

25. Robert H. Bell, "Bertrand Russell and the Eliots," *American Scholar*, Vol. 52, Summer 1983, p. 324.

26. Seymour-Jones, pp. 497–498.

27. Ann Pasternak Slater, "Vivienne Eliot's Biography," *Areté*, Winter 2001 <http://www.aretemagazine.com/t_article.jsp?id=46> (June 4, 2007).

CHAPTER 6. CAPSTONE OF THE POETRY

1. John Lehmann, "T. S. Eliot Talks About Himself and the Drive to Create," *The New York Times Book Review*, November 29, 1953, p. 5.

2. "Murder in the Cathedral," in *Collected Plays* (London: Faber & Faber, 1962), p. 43. "Burnt Norton," *Four Quartets, Collected Poems 1909–1962* (New York: Harcourt Brace Jovanovich, Publishers, 1963), p. 176.

3. T. S. Eliot, "Burnt Norton," *Four Quartets, Collected Poems 1909–1962*, p. 175.

4. Ibid., p. 176.

5. Ibid., p. 181.

6. Craig R. Whitney, "2 More T. S. Eliot Poems Found Amid Hundreds of His Letters," *The New York Times*, November 2, 1991, <http://select.nytimes.com/search/restricted/article?res=F20610FA355A0C718CDDA80994D94> (June 4, 2007).

7. Ronald Bush, *T. S. Eliot: A Study in Character and Style* (New York: Oxford University Press, 1983), p. 210.

8. Ronald Schuchard, "Burbank with a Baedeker, Eliot With a Cigar: American Intellectuals, Anti–Semitism, and the Idea of Culture," *Modernism/modernity*, Vol. 10, No. 1, 2003, p. 16.

9. Eric Ormsby, "On the Turning Away," review of Craig Raine, T. S. Eliot (Oxford: Oxford University Press, 2006), *New York Sun*, February 21, 2007.

10. Schuchard, p. 15.

11. Ibid.

12. Anthony Julius, *T. S. Eliot, Anti–Semitism, and Literary Form* (London: Thames and Hudson, 2003), p. 213.

13. John Lehmann, "T. S. Eliot Talks About Himself and the Drive to Create," *The New York Times Book Review*, November 29, 1953, p. 5.

14. Donald Hall, "T. S. Eliot," *Writers at Work: The* Paris Review *Interviews*, Second Series, Introduced by Van Wyck Brook (New York: The Viking Press, 1963), p. 101.

15. T. S. Eliot, "East Coker," *Four Quartets, Collected Poems 1909–1962*, p. 189.

16. Michael Coyle, "T. S. Eliot on the Air: 'Culture' and the Challenges of Mass Communication," *T. S. Eliot and Our Turning World,* Jewel Spears Brooker, ed. (New York: St. Martin's Press, LLC, 2001), p. 149.

17. T. S. Eliot, "Little Gidding," *Four Quartets, Collected Poems 1909–1962*, pp. 203–205.

18. Ibid., p. 204.

19. Ibid., p. 209.

20. Helen Gardner, *The Composition of Four Quartets* (London: Faber & Faber, 1978), p. 17.

21. Ibid., pp. 16–17.

22. A. Walton Litz, "Repetition and Order in the Wartime Quartets," in *Words in Time: New Essays on Eliot's Four Quartets*, ed. Edward Lobb (Ann Arbor: The University of Michigan Press, 1993), p. 181.

23. Ibid., p. 183.

24. Lyndall Gordon, *T. S. Eliot: An Imperfect Life* (New York: W. W. Norton & Company, 1999), p. 459.

25. Hall, p. 105.

26. Helen Gardner, *The Art of T. S. Eliot* (London: The Cresset Press, 1949), p. 2.

27. Helen Vendler, review of *The Waste Land: A Facsimile and Transcript of the Original Drafts* (New York: Harcourt Brace Jovanovich, 1971), *The New York Times Book Review*, November 7, 1971, p. 45.

28. Frank Kermode, "Reading Eliot Today," *Nation*, Vol. cxcvii, October 26, 1963, pp. 263–264.

29. T. S. Eliot, "To Walter de La Mare," in *Collected Poems 1909–1962*, pp. 219–220.

CHAPTER 7. THE POET AS PLAYWRIGHT

1. James Longenbach, "Ara Vos Prec: Eliot's Negotiation of Satire and Suffering," *T. S. Eliot: The Modernist in History,* ed. Ronald Bush (Cambridge, U.K.: Cambridge University Press, 1991), p. 59.

2. T. S. Eliot, "The Waste Land," in *Collected Poems 1909–1962* (New York: Harcourt Brace Jovanovich, Publishers, 1963), p. 60.

3. T. S. Eliot, *Collected Poems 1909–1962* pp. 34–35, 47–48, 49–50.

4. Ronald Bush, *T. S. Eliot: A Study in Character and Style* (New York: Oxford University Press, 1983), p. 81.

5. T. S. Eliot, "Sweeney Agonistes: Fragments of an Aristophanic Melodrama," in *Collected Poems 1909–1962*, pp. 111–124.

6. Ibid., p. 119.

7. Ibid., p. 122.

8. Peter Ackroyd, *T. S. Eliot: A Life* (New York: Simon and Schuster, 1984), p. 200.

9. Bush, p. 162.

10. T. S. Eliot, "The Three Voices of Poetry," in *On Poetry and Poets* (New York: The Noonday Press, 1961), p. 98.

11. E. Martin Browne, *The Making of T. S. Eliot's Plays* (Cambridge, U.K.: Cambridge University Press, 1969), p. 33.

12. T. S. Eliot, "Murder in the Cathedral," in *Collected Plays* (London: Faber & Faber, 1962), p. 46; Browne, pp. 35, 36.

13. T. S. Eliot, "Murder in the Cathedral," in *Collected Plays*, p. 26.

14. Ibid., p. 30.

15. Donald Hall, "T. S. Eliot," *Writers at Work: The* Paris Review *Interviews*, Second Series, Introduced by Van Wyck Brook (New York: The Viking Press, 1963), p. 102.

16. Michael Grant, ed., *T. S. Eliot: The Critical Heritage* (London: Routledge & Kegan Paul, 1982), p. 37.

17. Browne, p. 154.

18. Ibid., p. 90.

19. John Gross, "Review of 'The Family Reunion,'"

Sunday Telegraph, June 20, 1999, <http://members .aol.com/actorsite2/gh/reunion.htm> (June 4, 2007).

20. Browne, p. 342.

21. Helen Gardner, "The Comedies of T. S. Eliot," *T. S. Eliot: The Man and His Work*, ed. Allen Tate (New York: Delacorte Press, 1966), p. 181.

22. Edmund Wilson, "The First Waste Land—II," *The New York Review of Books*, Vol. 17, No. 8, November 18, 1971, <http://www.nybooks.com/articles/10387> (March 5, 2006).

23. Helen Vendler, review of *The Waste Land: A Facsimile and Transcript of the Original Drafts* (New York: Harcourt Brace Jovanovich, 1971), *The New York Times Book Review*, November 7, 1971, p. 45.

24. Myron Matlaw, *Modern World Drama: An Encyclopedia* (New York: E. P. Dutton & Co., Inc., 1972), p. 234.

25. Kai Bird and Martin J. Sherwin, *American Prometheus: The Triumph and Tragedy of J. Robert Oppenheimer* (New York: Alfred A. Knopf, 2005), p. 377.

26. Cynthia Ozick, "T. S. Eliot at 101: 'The Man Who Suffers and the Mind Which Creates,'" in *Fame & Folly* (New York: Alfred A. Knopf, 1996), p. 44.

27. Ibid.

28. T. S. Eliot, "The Cocktail Party," in *Collected Plays*, p. 213.

29. Lyndall Gordon, "Eliot and Women," in Bush, p. 12.

30. T. S. Eliot, "To My Wife," in *Collected Plays*, p. 294; *Collected Poems 1909–1962*, p. 221.

31. Hall, p. 100.

32. T. S. Eliot, "Rhapsody on a Windy Night," *Collected Poems 1909–1962*, pp. 16–18.

33. T. S. Eliot, *Inventions of the March Hare: Poems*

1909–1917, ed. Christopher Ricks (New York: Harcourt Brace & Company, 1996), p. xix.

34. Jack Kroll with Constance Guthrie, "The 'Cats' Meow on Broadway," *Newsweek*, October 11, 1982. Reprinted in *New York Theatre Critics' Reviews*, Vol. XXXXIII, No. 13, October 18, 1982, pp. 197–199.

35. Karen Christensen, "Dear Mrs. Eliot. . . ," *The Guardian*, January 29, 2005 < http://books.guardian .co.uk/review/story/0,,1400192,00.html> (June 4, 2007).

36. Michael Billington, "Theater in London: T. S. Eliot Becomes a Figure of Controversy," *The New York Times*, March 11, 1984, p. H1.

CHAPTER 8. THE POET AS CRITIC

1. James E. Miller Jr., *T. S. Eliot: The Making of an American Poet, 1888–1922* (University Park, Pa.: The Pennsylvania State University Press, 2005), p. 414.

2. Caroline Behr, *T. S. Eliot: A Chronology of his Life and Works* (New York: St. Martin's Press, 1983), p. 20.

3. Valerie Eliot, ed., *The Letters of T. S. Eliot*, Volume I, 1898–1922 (New York: Harcourt Brace Jovanovich, Publishers, 1988), p. 280.

4. T. S. Eliot, "The Perfect Critic," in *The Sacred Wood: Essays on Poetry and Criticism* (London: Methuen & Co Ltd, 1920), p. 11.

5. Ronald Schuchard, *Eliot's Dark Angel: Intersections of Life and Art* (New York: Oxford University Press, 1999), p. 216.

6. T. S. Eliot, *On Poetry and Poets* (New York: The Noonday Press, 1957), p. 117.

7. T. S. Eliot, "Hamlet and His Problems," in *Selected Essays, 1917–1932* (New York: Harcourt, Brace & World, Inc., 1960), p. 124.

8. Ibid., pp. 124, 126.

9. Ibid., p. 125.

10. Ibid., pp. 124–125.

11. Ibid., p. 125.

12. Ibid., p. 126.

13. Michael Grant, ed. *T. S. Eliot: The Critical Heritage* (London: Routledge & Kegan Paul, 1982), Vol. 2, pp. 370–371.

14. William Rose Benét, *The Reader's Encyclopedia*, 2nd ed. (New York: Thomas Y. Crowell Company, 1965), Volume Two, M–Z, s.v., "objective correlative."

15. William Rose Benét, *The Reader's Encyclopedia*, 2nd ed. (New York: Thomas Y. Crowell Company, 1965), Volume One, A–L, s.v., "dissociation of sensibility."

16. William Rose Benét, *The Reader's Encyclopedia*, 2nd ed. (New York: Thomas Y. Crowell Company, 1965), Volume Two, M–Z, s.v., "Tradition and the Individual Talent."

17. T. S. Eliot, "Tradition and Individual Talent," in *Selected Essays*, 1917–1932, pp. 11, 7, 10–11.

18. T. S. Eliot, "Ben Jonson," in *Selected Essays*, p. 137.

19. T. S. Eliot, "Shakespeare and the Stoicism of Seneca," in *Selected Essays*, 1917–1932, p. 117.

20. T. S. Eliot, "Yeats," in *On Poetry and Poets*, p. 299.

21. T. S. Eliot, "Tradition and Individual Talent," in *Selected Essays*, 1917–1932, pp. 3–4.

22. Ibid., p. 6.

23. Valerie Eliot, p. 617.

24. T. S. Eliot, "Tradition and Individual Talent," in *Selected Essays*, p. 5.

25. T. S. Eliot, "Philip Massinger," in *Selected Essays*, 1917–1932, p. 182.

26. T. S. Eliot, "Dante," in *Selected Essays*, 1917–1932, p. 212.

27. Epigraph to T. S. Eliot, *The Waste Land: A Facsimile*

and Transcript of the Original Drafts, ed. Valerie Eliot (New York: Harcourt Brace Jovanovich, Inc., 1971), unnumbered page.

28. T. S. Eliot, "Shakespeare and the Stoicism of Seneca," in *Selected Essays, 1917–1932*, p. 117.

CHAPTER 9. POET FOR OUR CENTURY?

1. Robert Giroux, "A Personal Memoir," *T. S. Eliot: The Man and His Work*, ed. Allen Tate (New York: Delacorte Press, 1966), p. 337.

2. Caroline Behr, *T. S. Eliot: A Chronology of his Life and Works* (New York: St. Martin's Press, 1983), p. 76.

3. E. Martin Browne, *The Making of T. S. Eliot's Plays* (Cambridge, U.K.: Cambridge University Press, 1969), p. 342.

4. Karen Christensen, "Dear Mrs. Eliot. . . ," *The Guardian*, January 29, 2005 <http://books.guardian.co.uk/review/story/0,,1400192,00.html> (June 4, 2007).

5. Browne, p. 342.

6. Behr, p. 86.

7. Richard Badenhausen, "Rethinking 'Great Tom': T. S. Eliot and the Collaborative Impulse," *T. S. Eliot and Our Turning World*, Jewel Spears Brooker, ed. (New York: St. Martin's Press, 2001), p. 180.

8. Ronald Schuchard, *Eliot's Dark Angel: Intersections of Life and Art* (New York: Oxford University Press, 1999), p. 251, footnote 340.

9. T. S. Eliot, *The Waste Land: A Facsimile and Transcript of the Original Drafts*, ed. Valerie Eliot (New York: Harcourt Brace Jovanovich, Inc., 1971).

10. Valerie Eliot, ed., *The Letters of T. S. Eliot*, Volume I, 1898–1922 (New York: Harcourt Brace Jovanovich, Publishers, 1988), p. xv.

11. Ibid., opposite the copyright page.

12. Caryn James, "The Dark Side of Genius and Its

Supporting Cast," *The New York Times*, December 2, 1994, <http://movies2.nytimes.com/mem/movies/review.html?r es=9407EED71E30F931A35751C1A962958260> (June 4, 2007).

13. Robert Alter, "What Was T. S. Eliot?" *Commentary*, March 1989, pp. 31–37.

14. "T. S. Eliot at 101," *The New Yorker*, pp. 119–154, November 20, 1989, reprinted in *Fame & Folly* (New York: Alfred A. Knopf, 1996), pp. 3–49.

15. Helen Gardner, "The Comedies of T. S. Eliot," in *T. S. Eliot: The Man and His Work*, p. 159.

16. David Barber, "The Artist as a Young Mandarin," *The Boston Globe*, Sunday, January 1, 2006, <http://www.boston.com/news/globe/ideas/articles/2006/01/01/the_artist_as_a_young_mandarin/> (June 4, 2007).

17. John Crowe Ransom, "Gerontion," in *T. S. Eliot: The Man and His Work*, p. 133.

GLOSSARY

allusions—References to other literary works.

chorus—Actors commenting on the main action of a drama.

couplet—Pair of rhyming verses.

dissociation of sensibility—A term coined by Eliot to describe a loss of fusion of thought and feeling that characterized English poetry after the age of the seventeenth-century metaphysical poets.

doggerel—Comic verse that is usually irregular in rhythm; also, crude verse.

dramatic monologue—A poetic form in which a single character addresses a nonspeaking listener, revealing aspects of his or her character and of the dramatic situation.

epigraph—A quotation used at the beginning of a book, chapter, or poem, chosen for its connection to what follows.

facsimile—An exact copy.

impersonality of the author—Eliot's insistence that what matters in literature is the work, not the life of its author; that a work achieves significance only insofar as the author transforms his or her personal experience into something universal.

literary modernism—A general term applied to a range of experimental and avant-garde styles in early twentieth-century literature.

objective correlative—A term coined by Eliot to define the words, events, or objects that evoke a particular emotion in a work of art.

occasional poem—A poem intended to mark a particular occasion.

original sin—The belief of many Christian denominations that human beings are born with an inclination to sin as a result of Adam's disobedience in the Garden of Eden.

pageant play—A dramatic form in which the history of a place or institution is portrayed through a series of scenes.

rag—Musical style, popular in America from about 1899 to 1917, incorporating elements of minstrel shows and African-American banjo music.

symbolism—A literary movement seeking to convey the experiences of inner life through carefully chosen images.

transcript—A written or printed copy.

Trinity, doctrine of—The belief that God exists in three persons: the Father, the Son, and the Holy Spirit.

Unitarian—A member of a liberal Christian denomination founded upon the belief that God is one being.

Major Works by T. S. Eliot

Poetry:

Prufrock and Other Observations (London: The Egoist Ltd, 1917).

Poems (London: The Hogarth Press, 1919).

Ara Vos Prec (London: The Ovid Press, 1920).

Poems (New York: Alfred A. Knopf, 1920).

The Waste Land (New York: Boni and Liveright, 1922; London: The Hogarth Press, 1923; London: Faber & Faber Ltd, 1962).

Poems, 1909–1925 (London: Faber & Gwyer Ltd, 1925; New York: Harcourt, Brace and Company, 1932).

Ash-Wednesday (London: Faber & Faber Ltd, 1930; New York: G. P. Putnam's Sons, 1930).

Old Possum's Book of Practical Cats (London: Faber & Faber Ltd, 1939; New York: Harcourt, Brace and Company, 1939).

East Coker (London: Faber & Faber Ltd, 1940).

Burnt Norton (London: Faber & Faber Ltd, 1941).

The Dry Salvages (London: Faber & Faber Ltd, 1941).

Little Gidding (London: Faber & Faber Ltd, 1942).

Four Quartets (New York: Harcourt, Brace and Company, 1943; London: Faber & Faber Ltd, 1944).

Collected Poems 1909–1962 (London: Faber & Faber Ltd, 1963; New York: Harcourt, Brace & World, Inc., 1963).

Plays:

Sweeney Agonistes (London: Faber & Faber Ltd, 1932).

The Rock (London: Faber & Faber Ltd, 1934; New York: Harcourt, Brace and Company, 1934).

Murder in the Cathedral (London: Faber & Faber Ltd, 1935; New York: Harcourt, Brace and Company, 1935).

The Family Reunion (London: Faber & Faber Ltd, 1939; New York: Harcourt, Brace and Company, 1939).

The Cocktail Party (London: Faber & Faber Ltd, 1950; New York: Harcourt, Brace and Company, 1950).

The Confidential Clerk (London: Faber & Faber Ltd, 1954; New York: Harcourt, Brace and Company, 1954).

The Elder Statesman (London: Faber & Faber Ltd, 1959; New York: Harcourt, Brace and Company, 1959).

Collected Plays (London: Faber & Faber Ltd, 1962).

Literary Criticism:

The Sacred Wood (London: Methuen & Co., Ltd, 1920; New York: Alfred A. Knopf, 1921).

Selected Essays, 1917–1932 (London: Faber & Faber Ltd, 1932, 1951; New York: Harcourt, Brace and Company, 1932, 1950).

The Use of Poetry and the Use of Criticism (London: Faber & Faber Ltd, 1933, 1964; Cambridge, Mass.: Harvard University Press, 1933).

On Poetry and Poets (London: Faber & Faber Ltd, 1957; New York: Farrar, Straus and Cudahy, 1957).

To Criticize the Critic and Other Writings (London: Faber & Faber Ltd, 1965; New York: Farrar, Straus and Giroux, 1965).

FURTHER READING

Books

Bloom, Harold, ed. *T. S. Eliot*. Broomall, Pa.: Chelsea House, 2003.

Moody, A. David. *The Cambridge Companion to T. S. Eliot*. Cambridge University Press, 1995.

Williamson, George. *A Reader's Guide to T. S. Eliot*. New York: Syracuse University Press, 1998.

Wisker, Alistair. *T. S. Eliot: A Beginner's Guide*. New York: Hodder Headline, 2001.

Internet Addresses

Poetry, Poems, Bios & More — T. S. Eliot

http://www.poets.org/poet.php/prmPID/18

TIME 100: T. S. Eliot

http://www.time.com/time/time100/artists/profile/eliot.html

Eliot Reading "Prufrock"

http://www.salon.com/audio/2000/10/05/eliot

INDEX